A Gift For

From

With the hope
that it inspires you
to pursue a dream
of your own.

THE
TRY

The Secret to Success
in Life and Career

JAMES P. OWEN

with Brigitte LeBlanc
and Marji Wilkens

Book Design by Nita Alvarez
Illustrations by Randy Glass

SECOND EDITON

Skyhorse Publishing books may be purchased in bulk at special discounts for sales promotion, corporate gifts, fund-raising, or educational purposes. Special editions can also be created to specifications. For details, contact the Special Sales Department, Skyhorse Publishing, 307 West 36th Street, Floor 11, New York, NY 10018 or info@skyhorsepublishing.com.

Visit our website at www.skyhorsepublishing.com

10 9 8 7 6 5 4 3 2 1

Second Edition ISBN: 978-1-62087-864-4
Created and designed in the United States of America; printed in China

Library of Congress Cataloging-in-Publication Data

Owen, James P.
 The try : the secret to success in life and career / James P. Owen.
    p. cm.
 ISBN 978-1-61608-117-1 (pbk. : alk. paper)
 1. Success--Case studies. 2. Successful people--Case studies.
 3. Determination (Personality trait) I. Title.
 BJ1611.2.O94 2010
 920.009′051--dc22
 [B]
                                    2010015453

CONTENTS

FEARLESS *No Obstacle Too Great*

RESILIENT *Lives Reinvented*

How I Stumbled on the Secret to Success

THIS BOOK had its beginnings on a blustery April day, when I found myself driving through a blinding rainstorm on the back roads of central Texas. I was out in the middle of nowhere with only the occasional small town or roadside stop to punctuate the seemingly endless miles of open plain. My destination: a ranch just outside the town of Stephenville — the home of Ty Murray, the legendary King of the Cowboys.

I'd been captivated by Ty's story from the moment I first heard it. At the age of three, when most little boys are still engrossed with their toys and teddy bears, Ty had set his sights on becoming the top rodeo cowboy of all time. For most of us, an audacious goal like that is never more than a childhood fantasy. But Ty was different. His vision became a driving ambition — one he pursued relentlessly until it was fulfilled at age twenty-eight, when he won a record-setting seventh title as the world champion all-around rodeo cowboy.

Ty's aspirations didn't stop there. As a young rodeo star intent on establishing bull riding as a sport in its own right, he co-founded the Professional Bull Riders, which he helped grow into a worldwide entertainment organization that brings events to millions of spectators around the globe. It seemed that he brought the same intensity and can-do attitude to everything he undertook, whether it was competing for a championship buckle, promoting the PBR, or training horses on his ranch.

Just what is it, I wondered, that drives someone like that? What's the winning principle that he has and the also-rans lack? And what can the rest of us learn from his example?

IN SEARCH OF THE WINNER'S EDGE

As I drove through the deluge, squinting to make out the road ahead, it wasn't hard to imagine the early pioneers who'd struggled to carve ranches and homesteads from this desolate-looking landscape. For them, the rule was "Do for yourself, or do without." These days, we eat takeout for dinner and take our cars to the shop for an oil change. If something breaks, we take it somewhere to be fixed or, more likely, simply go out and buy a replacement. I couldn't help thinking that all the comforts and conveniences we've gained could be robbing us of some skills and attitudes we may really need.

No sooner had I pulled up to the ranch house than Ty appeared in a slicker and boots. "The creek got so high it took down one of the fences," he said by way of a greeting. "Come on; we've got a job to do."

Soon I was standing on the slippery bank of a creek swollen with rushing water, as Ty instructed me to brace the fence post firmly against my shoulder. Intent on his task, he said almost nothing as he swiftly worked to refasten the downed strands of barbed wire. On the rodeo circuit, Ty was renowned for his focus and determination. Now I saw how he brought those same qualities to a routine chore. Drawn in by his concentration, I forgot all about the rain still falling around us.

Once we were dry and warm back at the house, I explained the reason for my journey. Ty was a great athlete; everyone knew that. But the odds dictate that even among the most gifted, hardest-working athletes, very few will ever become champions. What, I wanted to know, was the true secret of his success?

Ty looked up with a shy half-smile and answered, "My mom always said I was born with an extra supply of Try."

His words hit me like a thunderbolt.

In standard English usage, "try" is a verb that means "to make an attempt." But in cowboy culture, the word is a noun invested with profound meaning. When cowboys say, "That cowhand, he's got Try," they're talking about the quality of giving something every ounce of effort you can muster. And if a cowboy really, really admires someone, he'll say that person's got The Try — which means he or she is someone who always gives 110 percent and never, ever quits.

The Try. It was so simple…yet so powerful. If that idea could help propel Ty Murray to the pinnacle of his chosen field, what could it do for the rest of us?

Ty was quick to point out that The Try has little to do with winning medals, trophies, or any other kind of prize. As he says, no matter what the endeavor, you can never guarantee the quality of your performance, and you certainly can't guarantee the outcome. The only thing you can ever guarantee is that you'll "try your guts out." And if you do that, in his book you're a winner already.

To me, it seemed The Try was a "big idea" — one that might help a lot of people, and maybe even our country, to get through the tough times we're in. As I made the long drive home, I couldn't help wishing there were a way to bottle Ty's can-do spirit and dispense it to every person striving or struggling to get an education, find a job, run an enterprise, become fit, or battle a serious disease. Along the way, I would also want to impart The Try to every politician and civil servant in the country, from the White House on down.

HOW ORDINARY PEOPLE
DO EXTRAORDINARY THINGS

Energized and excited by my visit with Ty, I set out to find others like him — other people who've gone after their dreams with that same fierce inner drive. Once I opened my eyes to it, I realized that people with The Try are all around us. I'm not only talking about superstars like Michael Jordan or Oprah, who worked tirelessly for years to get to the top of their respective games. I'm talking about ordinary people who've tapped their own supply of Try to do some extraordinary things.

Out of all the remarkable people that I heard and read about, I picked an even dozen — Twelve with Try — who were willing to share their experiences and their insights into the inner dynamics of success. I wanted to know: Just what was it, deep down, that motivated them to put everything they had toward their dreams, no matter how tough the odds? How did they summon the will to keep forging ahead day after day, year after year? What tradeoffs did they make along the way? How did they define success? And what kept them going through those inevitable bleak moments when things went wrong and their confidence faltered?

What they had to say is distilled in this book's twelve real-life profiles. Flipping through the stories, you can see right away that The Try comes in many forms and flavors; there's no single recipe. It's a character trait that can be forged in a variety of ways, showing up among people of all ages, from all walks of life, and across many fields of endeavor.

In these pages you'll meet people who were driven by a childhood dream, like Ty Murray, or a long-held ambition, like Stacy Allison, who climbed Mount Everest.

But you'll also find some whose Try was ignited by a life-changing moment when they hit rock-bottom, found themselves headed for self-destruction, or came face-to-face with failure. As you'll read in the stories of Scott Silverman, Francisco Reveles, and Jerry Acuff, each one went through his own passage of fire and then found the inner strength to turn his life around.

In some people, like film director Lexi Alexander and social entrepreneur Ann Higdon, The Try grows from relishing a challenge and wanting to never let themselves down. Others are motivated by wanting to never let someone else down. Take, for example, the story of Brian Boyle, who fought his way back from the brink of death for the sake of his parents, and went on to realize a dream all his own. Still others find The Try when confronted by a need or challenge so compelling that they simply can't walk away. Jessica Jackley felt an urgent, irresistible push to find some meaningful way of easing global poverty. For Carlotta Walls LaNier, it came from a refusal to let racial discrimination stand in the way of her education. In the case of Julia Anderson, The Try meant holding her own against a debilitating disease. And for Hamse Warfa, The Try is what it took to survive war-torn Somalia and build a new life in America dedicated to helping others succeed.

Connecting the dots in these twelve stories, I also realized that The Try isn't just another self-help technique. In fact, it's not even something you can fully grasp intellectually. It's the kind of thing that can only come from the heart — a way of being that you cultivate and practice on a daily basis until it becomes a part of who you are. It's that burning desire to accomplish something, whatever it might be, coupled with the unshakable belief that *you can do it*.

Of course, you can never be assured of attaining your goal. We all have those times when we make an all-out effort and still don't win the prize. But in terms of earning respect and feeling genuine pride in yourself, whether you've reached your goal may be less important than what you put into the effort. In a very real way, The Try is its own reward.

MENTAL STRENGTH IS WHAT MATTERS MOST

Interestingly, there's a growing body of scientific evidence that, out in the real world, focus and effort often trump ability. That means IQ, talent, and physical strength may be less important to success than mental qualities such as discipline and perseverance.

One recent study of cadets at West Point, the elite military academy known for its ultra-rigorous program, found that those most likely to graduate weren't the smartest or strongest cadets, but those who most often demonstrated what you might call "grit" in their attitudes and behaviors. Other studies have found that elementary school children who are praised for their intelligence don't test nearly as well as children who are praised for their hard work.

You have probably heard Thomas Edison's famous observation that "genius is 1 percent inspiration and 99 percent perspiration." But did you know that Edison made more than 10,000 failed attempts to produce incandescent light before he invented the light bulb? At the point when Edison had logged more than 9,000 unsuccessful experiments, a young journalist asked him whether he felt like a failure and why he didn't give up. Edison replied, "Young man, why would I feel like a failure? And why would I ever give up? I now know definitively over 9,000 ways that an electric light bulb will not work."

IT'S ALL UP TO YOU

To my mind, The Try is what separates the doers and leaders among us from the dreamers and wannabes. A lot of people can come up with an idea for a great invention, a new product or company, or maybe even a novel or screenplay. But very, very few ever follow through with the months or years of hard work it takes to bring their ideas to fruition.

Let's face it: Ideas are a dime a dozen. You can be smart, you can be talented, and you still might not tap your true potential or fulfill your deepest ambitions. What makes things happen is putting *effort* behind your ideas, **actions** behind your words, and **intention** behind your dreams. That's what having The Try is all about.

So, instead of writing a book that leaves you wishing you, too, could do great things, I hope I've produced one that will help motivate and inspire you to *achieve* great things. I truly believe that if you've got The Try, anything is possible.

All it takes…is all you've got.

JAMES P. OWEN
Austin, Texas

RELENTLESS

The Will to Win

REALIZING A
CHILDHOOD DREAM

Ty Murray
King of the Cowboys

NOT MANY PEOPLE decide by the age of three what they want to achieve in life. Even fewer reach the pinnacle on which they've set their sights. Ty Murray is one of that rare breed. His story lends truth to the belief that "if you can dream it, you can do it."

Ty always knew that he wanted to be a rodeo champion. By the time his fifth-grade teacher asked him, "If you could do anything in the world, what would you do?" Ty was already fixed on his goal. What stoked the fires of his ambition was watching Larry Mahan, "the Babe Ruth of the rodeo," compete in the "roughstock" events — bareback, saddle bronc, and bull riding — the ones in which you literally risked life and limb with every crack of the gate. With six All-Around Cowboy World Championship titles, Mahan held the all-time record. Young Ty declared his intention to win seven.

Ty did start with some advantages, though not financial ones. The Murray family was of modest means, and their home was a trailer on the outskirts of Phoenix. But, coming from three generations of cowboys on both sides of his family, Ty seemed to have rodeo in his blood. He also had the love and support of his family, who never questioned his zeal. His mother, Joy, had been a rodeo competitor herself, and his father, Butch, a rodeo hand.

Most important of all, as Ty puts it, "My mom always said I was born with an extra supply of Try."

To say that Ty pursued his goal with single-minded determination hardly begins to describe it. Early on, he got the feel of things by riding calves out behind the trailer. When he was nine he rode his first bull, winning the Little Britches competition. By age twelve, he'd earned enough money helping his dad break wild horses to buy a mechanical bucking machine, which he nearly wore out. A few weeks later he won his first Junior Rodeo Championship despite a broken jaw. Earning the Arizona All-Around Junior Rodeo Championship nine times running, Ty turned professional as soon as he was eighteen, and at twenty became the youngest rider ever to win an All-Around World Championship.

"When I won my first world championship, it didn't feel like a big milestone," Ty remembers. "I didn't think, 'This year, I'm the best guy in the world.' I just felt like I was one step closer — one down, six to go."

What set apart Ty's brand of striving was not just how tirelessly he worked to advance his rodeo skills, but also the way he threw himself into any kind of practice that might help him compete. To improve his balance and coordination, he walked fence lines, learned to ride a unicycle, and took up juggling. For flexibility and strength, he trained in gymnastics, weightlifting, and martial arts. He also kept up his academics, attending Odessa College, where he made the Dean's List.

Through the early 1990s, Ty continued training and racking up championships. But inevitably, he encountered some setbacks on his way to the top of his sport. In 1995, plagued by knee injuries, he took a year off for surgery and rehab. He went back to competition and soon dislocated his shoulder; that meant more surgery, followed by more rehab. Then he dislocated the other shoulder.

"I realized that I'd spent a year doing nothing with my shoulder but lifting food to my mouth. If I'd been doing my usual rodeo training, I never would have injured it," recalls Ty. "So I hired a martial arts expert, a four-time national champion in Nippon Kempo, to train with me one on one. For all of 1997, we trained six days a week in his gym, which was an old meat locker with no AC and no heat. In the winter it was thirty degrees; in the summer, it had to be a hundred and twenty in there. He told me, 'The guys I beat trained in air conditioning.'

This is something that makes you tougher without your even knowing it. When I came back from that, I was in shape from head to toe."

In December, 1998, Ty achieved his life-long goal, earning a record-breaking seventh All-Around Cowboy World Championship title. Fittingly, it was his childhood hero, Larry Mahan, who presented him with the engraved trophy buckle.

While Ty is now retired from competition, he still brings his characteristic focus and determination to everything he does. He spends as much time as he can manage on his 2,100-acre ranch in Stephenville, Texas, a place that to him is "like Disneyland," where he works with his horses, builds fences, and is never, ever bored.

He stays active as an advisor to the Professional Bull Riders (PBR), which he and nineteen other riders founded in 1992, investing $1,000 each to create an athlete-owned organization that would raise the profile of "America's original extreme sport." The PBR has since grown into a multi-million-dollar sports powerhouse, sponsoring events that annually reach 1.5 million live spectators and 600 million broadcast viewers around the world.

You can also see Ty in action in recorded programs from season eight of ABC's *Dancing with the Stars,* a brand-new arena of competition for him. Although Ty practiced with his usual fervor, he and his partner did not end up as the winning team. At the close of the season Ty was, however, named the competitor who was "most improved."

LESSONS AND INSPIRATION

IT'S THE EFFORT,
NOT THE OUTCOME,
THAT MAKES YOU A WINNER

On this point, Ty is emphatic: *"When you climb down onto a bull, you can't guarantee you're going to stay on. You can't guarantee you're going to make a good ride, and you can't guarantee that you're going to be a high scorer or any of that. The one thing you can guarantee every time is that you will try your guts out. Whatever the outcome is, that's what it is. But to me, if you give it from the bottom of your guts, that equates to a good outcome. And if you do that every time, you're going to win a lot more than you lose."*

ALWAYS FOCUS
ON THE CHALLENGE
RIGHT IN FRONT OF YOU

"At the beginning of the year, every football team says, 'We want to win the Super Bowl, the Super Bowl, the Super Bowl.' But if you're not there 110 percent on the very first kickoff of the very first game — if you're not focused only on that kickoff and that play, it doesn't matter. The Super Bowl is not going to come into the picture anyway. You have to be right here, right now, every time, every day. If you're not always going back to putting one foot in front of the other, you won't get up that mountain, whatever it is."

WATCH THOSE
WHO MODEL A
WINNING ATTITUDE

In Ty's experience, determination is something you learn by example, not by being instructed. Everything he knows about competing, he says, he learned by watching his dad breaking horses: *"He was tough, he was fearless, and whatever arose, he overcame it. Those three elements aren't optional if you're going to be a professional rodeo cowboy. You can take all the technical skill, all the knowledge, teach somebody all the mechanics in the world, but if you don't have those three elements it doesn't matter. Those are the things you can't teach."*

LEARN TO LOVE
BEING PUT TO THE TEST

Until I met Ty, I'd always thought the peak moments in an athlete's career were the ones when he or she makes the winning move or gets up in front of a cheering crowd to accept a trophy. But Ty doesn't see it that way at all. For him, it's more about enjoying the contest itself, with all its dangers. *"When you're bull riding,"* he says, *"you get asked about eight million times, 'Why would you do this?' My answer is that it's just like learning to compete in basketball, when there's one second on the clock, and you're the guy trying to make the three-pointer, and your team is down by two. That's how it feels every time you ride a bull. And to me, that kind of competition is fun.*

"Don't get me wrong. I went through that process where I would get uptight and choke or I'd change things. How to deal with pressure is something you do have to learn. But when I look back at my career, one of the greatest moments was when I was going to break the record for the most All-Around titles. The most exciting time was right before I climbed onto my very last bull. You know? I remember thinking, 'This is that moment . . . the moment that you've played in your backyard since you were three years old.' The moment that anyone in the world who's ever dreamed of being a professional athlete grows up thinking and dreaming about. Relishing those moments, enjoying the ride and the competition, that's something that I learned to love and thrive on."

CONFRONT WHATEVER
IT IS THAT SCARES YOU

"With bull riding, the stakes are high every time, every minute, because of the danger of it. That's not only what makes people watch the sport. In my opinion, it's what makes people do this sport — to be able to take something that's scary and figure out how to stay focused and fluid. That's the real test . . . One of the most valuable things I saw with my dad, is if there was something that was scary or wild, something that most people would flinch from, my dad did the opposite of that — he always went right to it. I just watched that over and over. It's not like he would say, 'Hey, whenever something's scary, just go to it.' You know that wouldn't work. What made it work was that's what he always did. So when I got faced with something scary, I just automatically went to it."

MONEY ISN'T
THE MOTIVATOR

"So many times, success is judged by money. But for me, it was never about that. I wanted to be the world's best cowboy, but I never thought, 'I'm going to be rich and famous.' Cowboys aren't, for the most part. Rodeo was just something that thrilled me and excited me, and I even liked practicing and the challenge of it. To me, if you can find something in your life that you're passionate about and then figure out a way to eat from doing that . . . then you're a success. I truly believe that."

SUMMING UP

IF YOU'RE FEARLESS AND GIVE 110 PERCENT
TO WHATEVER YOU DO, NOTHING ELSE MATTERS.

For more on Ty Murray:

Murray, Ty, and Eubanks, Steve. *King of the Cowboys.* New York: Atria, 2007.

Murray, Ty, and Santos, Kendra. *Roughstock: The Mud, the Blood, and the Beer.* Austin: EquiMedia Corporation, 2001.

www.tymurray.com

www.pbr.com

VISUALIZE, PRACTICE, AND BELIEVE

LEXI ALEXANDER

Oscar-Nominated Film Director

SCENE: A sunny day in an industrial area of Long Beach, California. A bus pulls up and a woman steps off. Young and trim, with flowing, shoulder-length hair, she carries two duffel bags and a pair of boxing gloves, the only possessions she has on this side of the Atlantic. At the age of nineteen, she has traveled from her home village outside Heidelberg, Germany, to compete in the World Karate and Kickboxing Championship, where she has taken the top prize in the middleweight division. But it's Hollywood that lures her. On her face we see a half-smile and a look of anticipation. Lexi Alexander has decided to stay.

CUT TO: The 75th Annual Academy Awards ceremony, eight years later. Lexi's first film, *Johnny Flynton*, about a young boxer with a temper he can't control, has been nominated in the "best live-action short film" category. Accustomed to working on a shoestring, Lexi is decked out in borrowed jewelry and an evening gown designed and sewn by her friend, Tom Farrell, a teacher at the California Design College. She looks up nervously as the presenter for her category steps up to the mike. Jennifer Garner smiles, tears open the envelope, and ...

If it had been a movie, the next frames might have shown a beaming Lexi walking down the aisle of the Kodak Theatre to deliver her acceptance speech. But that's not how it happened. With four other nominees in her category, the Oscar was a long shot, like Lexi's whole career has been.

That's just how it is in Hollywood, especially for a woman who wants to direct films other than feel-good romantic comedies. Kathryn Bigelow's historic "best picture" and "best director" Oscar wins for *The Hurt Locker* put a chink in that glass ceiling but certainly didn't shatter it. "Hollywood is a complete boys' club," Lexi says with a crisp German accent. "When the studio CEOs think of a director, they think of a Spielberg or a Tarantino or a slick young guy like Spike Jonze. And they certainly don't think of women as directing action movies. It's just harder for us. But just because it isn't easy doesn't mean it's not possible."

It's no coincidence that two of Lexi's favorite movies are *Rocky,* the classic underdog tale, and *Rudy,* the story of a young man who is told he's too small to play football for Notre Dame.

Oscar Wilde famously observed that "life imitates art," and it seems that Lexi has spent her whole adult life playing out the story of the underdog who is knocked down and gets up over and over again.

Transcending obstacles has also been a core theme of the films she writes, produces, and directs. Her latest movie, *Lifted*, tells of the courage of a young Alabama boy whose world falls apart when his father is redeployed to military service in Afghanistan. Lexi's still looking for a distributor, even though audiences have loved the movie in test screenings. "When you're competing with huge studio movies, it's hard to get through the gatekeepers. It costs a lot to put movies in theaters, and what appeals to Middle America doesn't necessarily appeal to a Hollywood executive," says Lexi. "But I have to believe in miracles. I know someone out there will want people to see this movie."

Lexi credits her mother's reliance on positive thinking for her ability to believe in herself. "You can call it crazy New Age stuff if you want, but when I was thirteen and read books like *The Art of Positive Thinking* and *Creative Visualization*, it was an 'Open, sesame' for me. If you're a kid and haven't had a lot of negative experiences, you're not cynical. You just take in the message," says Lexi. "When I got off that bus in Long Beach, I had no connections in the US at all. Breaking into Hollywood should have been impossible. But because I kept visualizing myself being able to do it, I could. If you don't see a huge mountain in front of you, it's not there."

Her years of martial arts training, where "you can only master a kick if you do it 77,000 times," turned out to be another advantage for Lexi, helping her acquire habits of focus, effort, and discipline. To pursue her filmmaking dreams, she enrolled in acting school while attending classes in film directing, producing, and writing at UCLA. She financed it all by working as a stuntwoman on the side, which let her see the filmmaking process from the other side of the camera.

Lexi's 2003 Oscar nod helped her turn one of her original screenplays into a full-length feature film, *Green Street Hooligans*, which sets a story of friendship and loyalty in the violent world of British soccer. Starring the bankrollable Elijah Wood, the movie was released in 2005, earning critical acclaim, a slew of awards, and modest box office receipts.

After that, Lexi's agents and advisors all insisted that her next movie would have to be a studio film. If it were a hit, she'd have the bargaining power to do the kind of movies she wanted. She read the script for *Million Dollar Baby* and was ready to jump on it. But when Clint Eastwood made a bid for the project, she knew there was no way she could compete. She signed on to develop *Labor Day* for Disney and when that project fell apart, took on *Punisher: War Zone* for Lionsgate. Based on a vengeance-crazed Marvel comic book character, *Punisher* played well with its core demographic of teenaged boys, but still tanked at the box office.

"The opening weekend for my studio film, which failed so badly at the box office, was one of the toughest things I've ever faced. The week my movie came out, I had twelve scripts to consider. The week after, I had none. I thought, 'I'm finished; I have to pack my bags.' It took everything I had just to get out of bed…then another two or three months to see a way to go from there. But by month three, I was writing the script for *Lifted,* raising the money outside Hollywood, talking a lot of people into working for free, and getting ready to shoot the movie in Alabama," she says. "I didn't ask anybody in Hollywood. I just went ahead and made my movie."

At this point, Lexi doesn't even think about winning an Oscar someday. Her ambition is to simply be able to make movies consistently. That is, to be able to make the kinds of movies she wants to make. She no longer kickboxes — "I've got screws in both my knees," she reports — but has taken up medieval sword fighting to help keep the competitive juices flowing. Rather than taking it easy in between projects, she actively works at her career from 8 AM to 8 PM every day, whether she has a film in the works or not.

"Either I'm going to pack my bags and quit, or just keep going the same way I did when I first arrived here," she says. "There's nothing magical about it. This is what I do best, and I know I'm good at what I do. It's a gift, like having a gift for composing beautiful music. It's a damned hard life, but I'm not about to spit my gift in the face."

LESSONS AND INSPIRATION

JOB ONE IS TO
FIND YOUR GIFT

We all have different talents, Lexi believes, which means your first job is to discover your gift, whatever it may be. As she observes, *"People who do work within their calling have an advantage, because they don't have to work so much on their skill. They can concentrate on the tough part, which is sitting down and actually composing the music or writing the book. There are a lot of people with ideas. It comes down to the one who's going to write the screenplay."*

YOUTH AND INEXPERIENCE
CAN BE AN ADVANTAGE

Lexi admits that after years in Hollywood and countless rejections, it takes a bit more doing to apply positive thinking. But she still practices the techniques that helped her get started in Hollywood, when her innocence let her see more opportunities than obstacles. She likes to recall watching a talented eight-year-old as he demonstrated martial arts forms: *"This young boy did a three-sixty and then a double-axe kick in the air. I mean, imagine the best Cirque du Soleil athlete you've ever seen — this kid was just defying gravity! I asked his coach, 'How does he do it? What he's doing is just not possible.' The coach replied, 'Nobody ever told him he couldn't.'"*

DON'T BEG FOR HELP; BARGAIN FOR IT

"I used to get up at 6 AM and drive across town to be the personal trainer for a studio executive so he would be one of my mentors in the business," Lexi remembers. "I did it three times a week for free, and it was the best thing I ever did. He agreed to write a letter supporting my movie and that got me a lot of favors. I had to constantly figure out who could help me and what I could offer them. You can't think that you're entitled to help; it's also about what you can give. After all, it's a business!"

YOU'VE GOT TO HAVE A TOUGH SKIN

Lexi worries that her story might be discouraging to girls of a younger generation: "I don't want some young girl to read this and focus on how difficult the business can be. To do what I do, you have to go out every week and submit a project to people. I constantly have ideas and write scripts, and I can't count the number of rejections I've had. Some things work; a lot don't. You have to be able to take a lot in stride. But then, look at what's happened! We have a president nobody would have expected, and we have a female Speaker of the House. All kinds of stereotypes have been broken. Anything is possible — it truly is, as long as you don't focus on the obstacles."

BEING GENUINELY CONFIDENT IS THE BIGGEST CHALLENGE

"I'm consistently hard on myself, which makes me wonder, 'How is my energy when I walk into the room?' You can't fake confidence.

17

Confidence only comes from what you know to be the truth. If your subconscious believes you're a loser, people pick that up. You have to respect what you have achieved, even if you're not where you wanted to be."

DON'T SELL OUT
YOUR SOUL

Lexi was devastated when *Punisher* flopped at the box office, but the lesson from that very public failure is one she's taken to heart: *"The quality screenplays go to the famous directors; as a newcomer, you have to take the scraps. I thought I could make something out of the scraps, but it didn't work because it wasn't authentic to me. By compromising on the kind of work I was willing to do, I set my career back ten steps. I was knocked out and on the ground . . . but back on the count of eight."*

STAY OPEN
TO INSPIRATION

Success and its trappings can get in the way of new ideas, Lexi has found: *"When you start making films for studios, they tend to fly you first class. I enjoyed that, but from a storyteller point of view, there aren't as many stories in first class. When you're telling stories about real people, you belong back in coach, squeezed in between two other people. That was one of my secrets. In coach, you hear the most amazing things!"*

RESPECT YOUR
ACCOMPLISHMENTS
AS WELL AS YOUR AMBITIONS

"I don't feel like I've achieved anything," Lexi says, *"but other people tell me I've achieved more than anyone else they know. The one thing I know is that I'm not done learning and I'm not done achieving. I'm working on giving respect to what I've done in my life while still having the drive to do more."*

S U M M I N G   U P

ALL THINGS ARE POSSIBLE WHEN YOU COMBINE
POSITIVE THINKING WITH FOCUSED PRACTICE.

For more on Lexi Alexander:

www.lexialexander.com

http://articles.latimes.com/2003/mar/24/entertainment/et-baker24

REACHING BEYOND
THE LIMITS

STACY ALLISON

First American Woman to Scale Mt. Everest

YOU CAN'T GET any higher on this earth than Stacy Allison has been. On September 29, 1988, she became the first American woman to stand at the top of the world. Photographs show her triumphantly unfurling the American flag in a fifty-mile-per-hour gale at Everest's summit. You can see her relief and exhilaration upon completing the harrowing twenty-nine-day ascent.

What an admiring public didn't see was all the sweat and struggle leading up to this moment: the grueling climbs in Yosemite, Mt. McKinley, the Russian Pamir Range, and the Himalayas to build her technical skills; the punishing blizzards, heart-stopping avalanches, and many close calls in the "Death Zone" — the unforgiving territory above 19,000 feet. And the heartbreak of a failed attempt at Everest in 1987, when the worst storm in forty years trapped her climbing party for five days in a snow cave at 23,500 feet.

Mountaineering was something to which Stacy felt an almost magnetic attraction. From the time of her first rock climbing experience in Zion National Park, she was totally hooked by the feeling of being truly free, clear, and in the moment. As she got serious about it, mountain climbing also helped her realize that she could deal with the other challenging things in her life, like the searing emotional pain of an abusive marriage and tumultuous divorce.

Stacy started climbing seriously at the age of twenty-one and scaled Everest by the time she was thirty. In 1993, she led an expedition to K2, the second highest — and arguably most dangerous — peak in the world. Three in the team of seven made it to the top; Stacy and the others descended without reaching the summit after one climber fell to his death.

After that, she moved into a different phase focused on her family, motivational speaking, writing, and building the residential construction business she founded just before her successful Everest climb. She now has a thriving career, a happy second marriage, and two children, for whose sake she's given up climbing "big, dangerous mountains." But her mountaineering experiences have stayed with her. More than that, they have shaped her "go for it" approach to life. As she puts it, "Ambition is finding your talent and seeing how far it can take you. Ambition is doing what makes you feel most alive."

LESSONS AND INSPIRATION

IT'S ALL ABOUT YOUR MENTAL PUSH

A petite blonde who stands just five-foot-three, Stacy learned early on that the source of her physical prowess was in her mind — as were the limits to what she could do: *"In my early climbing experiences, I found out that I was really strong mentally. I could push myself beyond what I thought I was capable of doing … do things that I never really even considered. I thought, 'If I can do this, then maybe I can do something else that I never even considered.' It opened the door to possibilities I had yet to discover."*

YOU CAN ONLY ACHIEVE WHAT YOU CHOOSE

Stacy's story is a vivid reminder that great achievements come at great cost. To do anything exceptionally challenging, whether it's climbing a mountain or starting a company, you have to be prepared to commit yourself totally. Without that, it doesn't matter how heartfelt your dream may be. *"The goal is the starting point,"* says Stacy. *"If you don't believe in the goal you've set, and don't believe you can achieve it, you're not going to take the* risks to get there. At some point, you've just got to jump. You just have to let go of everything that has meant security to you and reach for that strength and courage deep down inside."

STRENGTH GROWS WHEN IT'S TESTED

Sometimes you have to reach a crossroads to know what you're capable of achieving. For Stacy, that defining moment was a life-or-death situation. She and a friend were climbing Mt. Robson, the highest peak in the Canadian Rockies, and got caught in a raging storm during the descent. They knew they couldn't expect any help, and there was a very real possibility they could die of hypothermia. Physically and mentally exhausted, Stacy's friend was on the brink of giving up. *"It was a moment of real clarity that I'll never forget. It wasn't just willpower; it was this very intense realization that this is how people die. I don't know where it came from, but it hit me in the face: This is my decision point. If I give up now, I'll die. In those situations, you have to keep moving. You have to put your mental strength to use and push yourself far beyond what you think you're capable of."*

LEARN HOW TO PUT FEAR ASIDE

"There's a time and place to recognize fear, to be anxious. But when you're actually making the moves on a rock face, you cannot let that fear surface. You can't focus on the risks or you'll start making mistakes. Yes, you always know the worst is possible; there are things you have no control over, like avalanches or rock slides. But you have to put it out of your head and do what needs to be done."

BREAK HUGE CHALLENGES INTO SMALLER ONES

As an example, Stacy points to the Khumba Ice Fall, the first major hazard Everest climbers encounter after leaving base camp. It's actually a glacier — a moving river of ice that drops off a 2,000-foot cliff. *"There's all the movement, the crashing, the creaking and moaning, the crevasses that are moving, the ice towers that tumble down. It's just too terrifying if you don't break it down into this step, that move, and then the next one."*

This lesson is one Stacy applies to many aspects of life: *"Say your company has been downsized and you've been fired. You've got to go out there and hit the streets — it's a scary thing! Sometimes the big picture is too overwhelming. To take the first step, you have to break it down into chunks — this day, this hour, this minute, I need to make one phone call or look at one job offering. After that, I can look at the big picture again, but then I'm going to have to go back to the next little thing I can do. That's a skill you can develop."*

FOCUS TAKES PREPARATION

Often we think of focus as an ability we can call forth anytime, simply as a matter of will. But Stacy learned that if you're not prepared, life can get in the way of the laser-sharp concentration it takes to navigate a treacherous mountain face: *"When you're on a mountain, you have to be focused on every step, every action, every decision, because every one has a consequence. So I think climbers become very good at compartmentalizing. You can't be thinking about what's going on at home — it's just too distracting."*

"On the other hand, if you're not dealing with the real issues and problems and challenges in your life, they will eventually take over. That means that when you leave to go climbing, you'd better make sure you have things in order," says Stacy. "If you've had an argument with someone, you clear that up before you leave. You let the people you love know that you love them. You don't leave things hanging. I believe that's true in any profession. If you don't deal with your issues, eventually they will surface and distract you from your focus."

GRAB HOLD OF YOUR PASSION, IF YOU'RE LUCKY ENOUGH TO FIND IT

"Climbing is what touches my soul, what moves my spirit. I don't know why that is ... I feel very fortunate that I found my passion, because I think most people never do. I also believe we only get one shot at true passion in our lives. We can enjoy many things, love to do many things, but that one thing that just gets us at a gut level, heart level, soul level — I think we only get one shot at that."

DARE TO TRY

Stacy's story made me wonder why most of us never discover that one passion that is so powerful and consuming, that it can drive us past any obstacle. What stands in the way of our finding the one thing we love to do? *I think it's the fear of failing and the fear of not fitting in,* Stacy says. "We want to be like everyone else, and we get so tied to things being a certain way. But when you're concerned about fitting in, you really narrow your options in life.*

26

I always tell my kids, if you're interested in something, try it. Even if you end up deciding it's not for you, it doesn't matter as long as you learn something."

THE ONLY REAL FAILURE IS GIVING UP

Painful as it was when Stacy failed in her first attempt at Everest, she took it in stride because she knew she'd be back: *"Climbing has helped me all my life because it taught me that it's okay to fail. I'm not afraid to fall flat on my face. I know I'm going to come back with a better idea of what to do the next time. Only when you give up does failure become permanent."*

S U M M I N G   U P

RECOGNIZE YOUR MENTAL STRENGTH
AND YOU WILL FIND YOU ARE CAPABLE OF
MUCH MORE THAN YOU EVER IMAGINED.

For more on Stacy Allison:

Allison, Stacy. *Many Mountains to Climb: Reflections on Competence, Courage, and Commitment.* Kansas City: Bookpartners, 1999.

Allison, Stacy, and Carlin, Peter. *Beyond The Limits: A Woman's Triumph on Everest.* Kansas City: Bookpartners, 1999.

VISIONARY

Driven by a Higher Purpose

"THEY TOLD US
WE WERE CRAZY"

JESSICA JACKLEY
Co-Founder, KIVA

WHEN SHE STARTS talking about Kiva, the global microlending organization she conceived and co-founded with her former husband, Matt Flannery, Jessica Jackley's enthusiasm is contagious. Her voice rises, her speech accelerates, and her eyes dart around the room. Her rapid-fire talk is peppered with laughter and expressions like "wow," "gosh," and "yay."

You can see how, while still in her twenties, Jessica managed to become one of the pioneers in a paradigm-shifting approach to global poverty — and did it in spite of all the experts who said it couldn't be done. She seems to be propelled by boundless energy and an unshakable belief in what she's doing. Those qualities endow her with the kind of confidence it takes to keep an idea moving forward, despite the obstacles.

Kiva is a nonprofit enterprise based on the principle that a little bit of money can make a huge difference in the lives of third-world entrepreneurs who are struggling and striving to get ahead. Through Kiva's website, www.kiva.org, individual lenders connect with people building small ventures in developing nations: a Philippine mother with a bread delivery business, an electronics repairman in Bolivia, a Guatemalan woman who sells natural medicines, a Tanzanian poultry farmer . . . the list goes on. Over time, the loans are repaid in full, so people who want to help can recycle the same capital to fund several budding entrepreneurs rather than just one. Presently the average loan is a little under four hundred dollars, and the repayment rate is an astonishing 98.4 percent!

The beauty of Kiva is that it turns people who live worlds apart into business partners with a genuine human connection. In the process, it transforms the usual donor/recipient roles into a relationship with dignity and accountability. Yet, when Jessica first started exploring the idea, nearly everyone she consulted said it could never work. The investment bankers said the enterprise wasn't scalable and would never be self-supporting. The foundation executives insisted no one would send money without getting a tax deduction. One lawyer friend even thought it might be illegal. But, finding no laws that prohibited what they had in mind, Jessica and Matt decided to just do it.

That was in 2005. Since then, Kiva has enabled over $100 million in loans to more than 314,000 borrowers — about 82 percent of them women — in 194 countries. It has been endorsed by Oprah and praised by Bill Clinton, along with many other notable supporters. In the process, Kiva has shown what microlending can do, and what a couple of dedicated people can do when they put their minds to it.

LESSONS AND INSPIRATION

GIVE YOUR PASSION THE TIME
IT NEEDS TO DEVELOP

The seeds of Jessica's passion were planted during her senior year in high school, when she went to Haiti with a church youth group and worked in an orphanage for a week. It was the first time she'd ever seen abject poverty. A few weeks after returning from her trip Jessica attended her school's senior prom, a full-on suburban version, complete with black-tie evening wear and limousines. *"I thought, 'You've got to be kidding me,'"* Jessica remembers. *"This is the same world, the same planet, just a short plane ride away from the people I met in Haiti. How can our lives be so very different? As I started to ask, 'How can this be possible?' I felt totally paralyzed. It was so overwhelming, knowing that not just a few people live like the people in Haiti, but many, many — in fact, most of the world. Painting the walls of an orphanage in Haiti was fine, but it didn't even make a dent. And I didn't know what would."* That feeling of having no clear direction persisted through Jessica's years at Bucknell College, where she studied philosophy to help illuminate the big questions, and political science to explore ways of solving big problems: *"All the ways I could figure out to get involved seemed arbitrary. What could a random middle-class white girl from Pittsburgh, Pennsylvania, do? Who was I to think I could go somewhere and help? I had all these issues."*

'TRUST THE "AHA" MOMENTS

Thinking back on her high-school trip to Haiti, Jessica recalls, *"The best moments of that trip were the moments of real connection, when I would sit down with someone my age or a little younger, and we would communicate in some way...those moments were really powerful to me. But I didn't know how that could solve anything."*

The pivotal moment came while Jessica, fresh out of college, was working at Stanford University. There she heard a talk by Muhammad Yunus, the Bangladeshi economist who developed the concept of microfinance. In 1976, he founded the Grameen Bank to provide small loans to poor borrowers who could not otherwise get credit. In 2006, Yunus and Grameen Bank were jointly awarded the Nobel Peace Prize, the first time a business corporation had been so honored.

"The way [Yunus] told his story was so cool. He walks into a village, sits down, talks with people, and hears that they are stuck in the cycle of lending. He reaches into his pocket for a few dollars, and the rest is history," says Jessica. *"It was so beautiful and do-able.*

He made it seem so possible because it is possible. I thought, 'I can do that. I can talk to people; I have a few dollars I can lend. I want to do what he did.' So I quit my job at Stanford and decided, 'Let's go do this.'"

INEXPERIENCE DOESN'T HAVE
TO BE AN OBSTACLE

Many of us hesitate to take even the first step in the pursuit of our dreams. Why? Because we feel untrained, unprepared, and lacking in credentials. But Jessica believes that the youth and idealism she and Matt brought to their work actually operated in their favor: *"When we were beginning, if we'd had any sense of how hard it would be, we would have been a lot more intimidated. But we weren't thinking, 'Let's start this global organization.' We were thinking about doing one thing to help our friends in a particular village. We wouldn't have been able to innovate the way we did without the fresh perspective and naïveté."*

At the same time, Jessica and Matt, who brought a technological focus to the venture, both worked tirelessly to fill their knowledge gaps. For example, they spent nine months just researching the logistics of international peer-to-peer lending. Deciding that she needed to know more about how business worked, Jessica enrolled in Stanford's MBA program and continued her studies while starting Kiva. It also helped that, being as passionate and engaged as she was, Jessica had no compunction about asking anyone for information or help. *"I really went overboard on this, as I have all my life,"* she admits.

"Basically, I information-interviewed anyone who would talk to me. I would say, 'Please, I will treat you to coffee. Just talk to me for five minutes!'"

THE RIGHT MENTORS CAN FUEL YOUR MOMENTUM

A key figure in the birth of Kiva was Brian Lehnen, founder of the Village Enterprise Fund, a nonprofit that helps people of East Africa start and grow small businesses. Impressed by Jessica's excitement about the group's work, Brian gave her a three-month job following up on grant recipients in Kenya, Uganda, and Tanzania. This provided her with an inside look at how a microfinance nonprofit worked, plus added reinforcement of her dream: *"I talked with entrepreneur after entrepreneur, and every single one of their stories was interesting and beautiful and triumphant, even if the business had failed. It seemed obvious to me that if more people in the world heard these stories — oh my gosh, the world would certainly become a different place."*

A different kind of mentor was Jim Patell at Stanford Business School: *"I especially remember one time when we were talking in the cafeteria and I got emotional and started to tear up. I said, 'I'm so sorry; I need to be more professional about this stuff.' He said, 'Jessica, let me tell you something. Professionals take it personally, like you take it personally, because you care. That's okay. It's a great thing to be invested in this heart and soul.' He gave me a lot of good encouragement about how to hang in there with something that was hard. That kind of life advice stuck with me even more than the technical advice."*

KEEP THE NAYSAYERS IN PERSPECTIVE

"When we would walk into an office of some expert or the leader of some big nonprofit, we'd say, 'Hey, we've got an idea! We want to lend money to our seven friends in Uganda. What do you think?' People would always jump to all these conclusions and assumptions — it's not scalable, it would be too expensive to take pictures of all the borrowers, and who's going to want to loan?

"We didn't know how to work all these things out, but we knew we would keep pursuing it. Matt would start thinking five or ten years out, and I'd say, 'You know what? Tomorrow Joseph is going to buy a new goat. We'll get his update online — won't that be fun?' We also knew we had something other people didn't. We had been in the middle of Uganda with the goat herder. We didn't know on Day One how we would change the world. But this was a project we could do, one little bit at a time."

MOVE BEYOND OLD WAYS OF THINKING

In Jessica's mind, the most critical roadblock to surmount is the mindset that gets in the way of seeing ourselves and others as human beings who share the same needs and potential. As she puts it, *"The most important thing about Kiva is that it can change the way that human beings see each other. It can change what we really believe is possible for ourselves and other people … and if I can truly be open enough to believe that human potential and intelligence is evenly distributed around the world, then this woman I'm talking to, who has never been to school, is just as smart,* or smarter, than me, and had she been given the opportunities I've had in my life, I'd be working for her.

"I think we're so hamstrung, so stuck in a lot of false paradigms that feel very safe to us. Like, 'I'm a member of the club of people in the world who are wealthy and supposed to be givers, not receivers, and there's a person out there who's needy and waiting for me to swoop in and do something to help them.' No! I can't tell you how many times during my travels, I've been the one in a position of need."

UNDERSTAND YOUR
TRUE MOTIVATIONS

With all the success Kiva has had, for Jessica the work is still driven by the power of person-to-person connections that bridge very different ways of life: *"The thing that I still care about most is not the money going back and forth. That's all very nice and very interesting, but it's a means to the end of this deeper connection, and that's the stuff I really care about."*

IF YOU TRULY HAVE A "BIG IDEA,"
GIVE IT TO THE WORLD

"When you build a tool, there's no way to anticipate how the world will use it. It's gone way beyond our wildest dreams," says Jessica. *"Still, you just need to stay focused on getting stuff done. You never feel like you've reached success. There's always so much more to do."*

SUMMING UP

IF YOU BELIEVE IN YOUR DREAM,

ALL THE "NO"S IN THE WORLD

CAN'T STOP YOU.

For more on Jessica Jackley (formerly Jessica Flannery):

www.jessica-jackley.com

www.kiva.org

www.poptech.org/popcasts/jessica_flannery__poptech_2007

TURNING HARDSHIP
INTO LEADERSHIP

HAMSE WARFA

Advocate for Peace

IT SOUNDS LIKE a scene from the movie *Black Hawk Down*. A young Somali boy watches, wide-eyed, as his family hastily loads a few possessions onto a truck, preparing to flee the bloody civil war that has erupted just a few miles from their home in northern Mogadishu. Though only eleven, he understands that the conflict is ending the secure life he's known. So when a band of students goes by, saying, "Come with us; we're going to stop the war," he slips away to join them without saying a word to anyone. He has no way of knowing that the demonstrators are walking right into the worst of the fighting.

For Hamse Warfa, the events of that day are still all too real. "The opposition is shooting at us, the government is shooting at us, there are explosions on both sides. We are all screaming and running back and forth," he remembers. "Even at that age, I was sure that this was my last day on earth."

Numb with shock, Hamse somehow managed to get away, jumping onto a truck as it lurched away from the carnage. Meanwhile, his panicked family waited at home, desperate to escape the spreading anarchy, but refusing to leave him behind. By the time he finally arrived, his family had only a few moments to rejoice and scold him at the same time. They took flight toward the Kenyan border, not knowing if they could ever return.

It took the Warfas a month to make what was normally a two-day trip, as the truck zigzagged around conflict zones and traversed bumpy back roads. In Kenya, the family arrived at a tent camp already teeming with thousands of refugees. The refugee camp soon proved to be nearly as dangerous as the chaos of their homeland. Fights broke out in lines where people spent five or six hours a day waiting for drinking water. Robbery and rape were everyday occurrences. Kenyans living nearby attacked the camp in attempts to drive out the refugees. Hamse's young cousin was killed.

Still, the Warfas were among the lucky ones. After surviving three years in the camp, they were able to seek asylum in the United States. In the winter of 1994, as the family boarded a plane bound for Colorado, Hamse could at last look forward to a new life. He had no idea of the hurdles still ahead.

Arriving in Denver, the family was met by below-freezing temperatures and hillocks of snow — a sight so exotic that Hamse's sister mistook them for salt. Chillier still was the reception the Warfas got from some of their mostly Caucasian neighbors. A campaign of slashed tires and smashed windows went on until the family moved again, to San Diego, where a community of Somalis had grown around military training programs at Camp Pendleton.

When Hamse arrived for his first day at Crawford High, he could speak only a little English, "mostly the bad words," he wryly remembers. But he didn't let that deter him. He had a natural sociability that went along with having fourteen siblings, plus a keen interest in sports developed around the dusty, improvised basketball court at the refugee camp. By making friends, playing hoops, and spending hours in the school library, Hamse learned English faster than anyone else in his family.

Money was a perennial concern. The once properous Warfas arrived in the United States with nothing more than they could carry. "The family expected me to contribute, rather than their contributing to me," Hamse says. "By the time I started at San Diego City College, I was trying to work, go to school full-time, and finish a degree as quickly as I could. It was really tough."

Hamse could have dropped out and made a living as a cab driver or cook, like so many refugees before him. But in his family, getting an education was an imperative, not an option. As he says, "I have six brothers, all of whom I knew would pursue an education. I wasn't about to spend the rest of my life as the only one without a degree."

He earned an associate degree in computer information systems, enrolled at San Diego State, and then hit a period of struggling to find his direction. He had contemplated pharmacy school, physics, computer science, public administration, and business, but he couldn't see any of those career paths as his life's work. As he floundered, his grades suffered, and he felt his dream of a quality education slipping away.

What did grab his interest was rallying people to work for peace and help those displaced by war. While still in high school, he had created the African Student Union. Finding no organized community of his countrymen when he got to San Diego City College, he started the Somalia Student Union there. Still, he doubted his abilities to be a leader who would have a real impact.

It was when he landed in San Diego State's political science department that Hamse began to see his future taking shape. He was riveted by the discussions and the coursework for classes such as "The Conduct of American Foreign Policy" and "Political Violence." After graduation, he continued his volunteer work with the refugee aid group, Horn of Africa Community in North America.

Then came 9-11. That, and the Iraq War that followed, ignited the passion behind Hamse's strengthening sense of purpose. He felt propelled by the same urgent drive for peace that had spurred him to join that ill-fated march as a young boy watching his country implode.

"After 9-11, my activism really came out because there was so much ignorance about the Muslim world. Here you have a population of 1.3 billion who are followers of a religion. All of a sudden, because of the actions of nineteen people, those 1.3 billion people are characterized as terrorists. In fact, it's this population that's more impacted by terrorism than anyone else. Al Qaeda kills more members of the Islamic faith than of any other religion," he says, his eyes flashing.

Hamse has since found many ways to aid refugees while working for peace at a high national and international policy level. "It's just senseless to see people killing other people," he states matter-of-factly.

As a program officer with Alliance Healthcare Foundation, Hamse manages grants and provides technical assistance to refugee-owned businesses. Based on the idea that peace starts with accurate information and understanding, in 2008 he launched the Institute for the Horn of Africa Studies and Affairs (IHASA), a research organization advising US policymakers on conflict resolution and prevention. IHASA has quickly gained credibility for its expertise on Horn of Africa issues, and Hamse is frequently called upon to help educate legislators and staff on Capitol Hill. He also has been asked to testify before Congress. "We are hopeful that our efforts here in the US will produce the desired results of peace with justice for the entire population in the Horn of Africa," he says.

Hamse's passion for peace is also expressed locally through free training programs for local youth. "No one has more energy and desire to improve the world than young people," he asserts. "My goal is to teach them how to be better advocates for their communities."

Meanwhile, Hamse has continued to pursue his education, but with a newfound intensity. He has earned a master's degree and two advanced certificates from the Congressionally-funded US Institute of Peace. He also found time to get married just two weeks after he completed his degree. Right now, he's busy organizing the next in a series of IHASA conferences on the region. He is also working toward a PhD. And he's just thirty-one years old!

"What really motivates me is that decades from now, if I'm alive, I want to be able to look back and say that I have done something beyond putting food on the table," Hamse says. "If you contribute something to humanity and make a difference in the lives you touch, you might have less money and fewer material things, but you won't miss them. You'll be living well inside. You'll have a successful life."

LESSONS AND INSPIRATION

EDUCATION
OPENS DOORS

Raised in a family that put the accent on education, Hamse came to America eager to learn. In his volunteer work, he also saw firsthand the plight of refugees who were educated and prominent in their native land, but found themselves "nobodies" in the United States, relegated to menial jobs in a country where they couldn't even speak the language. From his first high school days, he knew that academic studies would be his stepping-stone toward success. His advice is simple: *"If you want to succeed in life, education is the way to go."*

THE PATH TO YOUR IDEAL CAREER
MAY NOT BE A STRAIGHT LINE

Financial pressures were a big motivator for Hamse to earn a degree and to embark on his professional life as quickly as possible. Even so, he took the time to explore several career paths until he found one connecting with the things he really cared about. He didn't settle for something less just for the sake of getting a paycheck sooner.

VOLUNTEERING CAN
OFTEN BE A WAY IN

While still in college, Hamse put in many hours a week as a volunteer for the Horn of Africa Community in North America. There, he discovered his passion for community work, playing many organizational roles — from seeking grants and teaching English to helping refugees seek US citizenship. Not only did these experiences give him a strong base of management skills, they also led to a series of paid positions. Within a year after going on the payroll, he became the group's associate executive director, helping to oversee all programs.

ALWAYS HAVE A PLAN

Knowing your passion isn't enough, Hamse believes. You also need a plan for harnessing your energy and drive to accomplish something that matters. *"One thing that really always helped me was taking seriously the proverb, 'Those who fail to plan, plan to fail.' Sometimes your plans don't work out as you want; sometimes they do,"* he says. *"But I do know that if I had not set goals for myself and had a plan to achieve them, I probably wouldn't be able to do the kind of policy work I am involved in now, or to have as much influence."*

YOU CAN BE A LEADER AT ANY AGE

Although Hamse didn't think of himself as a leader when he first came to the United States, his strong sense of community and his empathy for other refugees soon led him to step in where he saw unmet needs. Both in high school and in college, he created student organizations to provide a forum and a resource for African students. These early experiences not only helped him recognize his own leadership potential, they also launched him on the road to becoming a respected figure in the policy arena.

LOOK BEYOND YOURSELF

Focused above all on preventing more bloodshed in his native land, Hamse also sees his work as an expression of the Somali spirit and tradition: *"Part of the collective identity of the Somalis is that you always have to think not just of yourself, but of your family, your cousins, your community. Thinking of the family or clan is so much a part of our culture. It's well known in our country that the explorers who came to Somalia in the 1600s told stories of the hospitality they received there. Even if the family were poor and had only a small amount of milk, they would give the last of it to a visitor. This collective identity has always been strong in my family, and in me."*

NEVER UNDERESTIMATE YOUR ABILITY TO CHANGE THINGS

"Some of my friends say that, basically, I'm nuts to work for change in Africa. They tell me, 'You can't do anything about it. Why would you even try?' Well, I believe the outcome is not something that we can determine today. It doesn't even belong to us. What belongs to us is our role today and how we can influence things for the better," Hamse says. *"Never give up hope."*

SUMMING UP

PERSONAL HARDSHIP CAN HELP YOU GROW —
AND GIVE YOU THE FOUNDATION FOR
CAREER AND LIFE SUCCESS.

For more on Hamse Warfa:
www.ihasa.org/
http://sandiegometro.com/2009/09/10th-annual-40-under-40-awards/

DO YOUR BEST, AND OPPORTUNITY WILL COME

ANN HIGDON

Founder, ISUS Charter Schools

NOBODY EXPECTED Ann Higdon to amount to much. Growing up in post-World War II Harlem, Ann was the child of a violent and abusive father and a mother who didn't have the will to leave him. She was periodically homeless from the age of four through her teens. Things were so bad that Ann took to sleeping with a knife under her pillow.

Mirroring the "don't-care" posture common in her harsh surroundings, she kept her hopes and dreams blanketed beneath a surly attitude, smart mouth, and poor academic performance. But deep inside, Ann admits, "I used to pretend I was a person with ability. In my fantasies I was brilliant, successful, and wonderful. When my father would tell me, 'you'll never amount to nuthin',' I would say to myself, 'I do amount to something, and I know I am going to be great. People are going to hear about me someday.'"

That kernel of stubborn pride and self-worth lay buried through Ann's early school years, even though it was obvious all along that she was exceptionally intelligent — so much so that her elementary school teachers had her skip two grades. Ann did not appreciate the recognition. "It was not a popular thing to be bright, and the kids teased me," she said. "I was so relieved when a new child came to our school who did better on the IQ test than I did. Then they finally left me alone."

But one day when she was nearly through high school, Ann was awakened to her abilities. A teacher passed back a graded essay, and across the top of Ann's paper was large, bold lettering that exclaimed: "You are profound and eloquent!" The praise lit up Ann's world. "I kept that paper for years until it was old and yellow. Those words meant the world to me."

Financial necessity was the other thing that stoked Ann's nascent ambitions. Having started high school at the age of twelve, she was out and on her own by sixteen, working to support herself and her sick mother while trying to get into college. With her spotty school record, Ann didn't qualify for an academically rigorous school. Through sheer persistence she gained provisional acceptance to a small Indiana college whose administrators made it clear they didn't expect her to do very well. But Ann saw low expectations as an invitation to prove what she could do. "Once I got there and saw that they graded on a curve, I decided I'd try to set the curve in all my classes, just to make the point that you shouldn't take people for granted."

Over time, the way Ann saw herself and her opportunities jelled into a clear philosophy of life — one she would eventually translate into an educational approach giving a fresh start to thousands of students at risk of falling through society's cracks. She had a way of gravitating to challenges and grabbing at every chance to improve her skills. Driving it all was the determination to do her best at whatever she tried.

After failing at a business she started and losing an investor's stake, Ann asked what kind of work she might do to repay the money. "It was accounting and tax work, not things I had any interest in," she says. "But as long as I had to do it, I was determined to do it well." She read everything she could about tax preparation, organized a bookkeeping system, and became skilled on the calculator, becoming an invaluable part of the business in the process.

Along the way Ann married, had four children, and eventually divorced. As a single mother and the sole supporter of her family, she worked hard to climb the career ladder. She traveled on weekdays to work on the East Coast, where the job opportunities were better, while her family was anchored in Dayton, Ohio, where the cost of living was lower. Intent on figuring out some way she could live and work in Dayton, she read an article about the government's problems with counterfeit food stamps and came up with an idea well ahead of its time: Why not replace food stamps with an electronic smart card?

"Everybody told me I couldn't do it — that if it could be done, someone smarter than me would have already done it," she says. "But that just strengthened my resolve." Undaunted by the bureaucratic maze, Ann crafted a proposal with a private-sector partner, presenting it to the US Department of Agriculture as a pilot program to be tested in the Dayton area. Ann worked with three levels of government to get the program off the ground, ultimately transforming the way the food stamp program is run.

Looking back on her life, Ann now sees the earlier stages of her career as the path leading her to launch Improved Solutions for Urban Systems (ISUS) and the charter schools that defined her purpose and ignited her passion. One day, she was talking with a regional bank president who asked if she had ideas to make the bank's federally mandated program of community investment more effective. As Ann recalls, "He told me, 'I don't mind helping, but I wish we weren't pouring money down a black hole. I just don't see the return. We'd like to be a player in the community and do something important, but we don't know what that should be.' So I started to research the opportunities."

Dayton's high-school dropout rate, then running at about 60 percent, attracted Ann's attention. "Very few people understand all the wounded places that need to be healed when you've been homeless, or abused, or rejected," she says. "The truth is, traditional education just does not work for so many troubled teens. What if I could find a way to give these kids another opportunity — another chance at education? I decided that it was a good fight and I wanted to get in it."

ISUS is indeed a different approach — one putting into practice Ann's pragmatic philosophy of being the best at whatever you do. "Most people only try to be average. So the idea is that if you do your best, you'll stand out from the crowd. Would you want to go to a mechanic who only knows 60 percent of what it takes to fix your car? Or a nurse who only understood 75 percent of the coursework? You don't have to be a brain surgeon; you can be a patient-care technician. But be the best patient-care technician around and opportunities will come to you."

Depending on funding levels, the four nonprofit programs under the ISUS umbrella serve 300 or 400 students at a time — all young people of whom society expects little. They enter the program, in Ann's words, as "over-age, under-achieving, non-attending, court-involved, disciplinary-problem dropouts." ISUS turns that around by expecting a great deal from them while giving them a place where they can feel safe and earn respect. Every student works toward a high-school diploma while learning job skills in computer technology and manufac-turing, healthcare, or construction. And there's zero tolerance for drugs, weapons, or violence. "If you're addicted and you want to come to ISUS, we'll save you a spot while you go through treatment," Ann explains.

Emblematic of the ISUS approach is the construction program, where students don't just learn how to build basic tract houses; they learn how to build award-winning homes that combine historically-accurate period detail with the latest in green technologies. Instead of competing for a dwindling supply of minimum wage jobs, ISUS students are busy equipping themselves for industries of the future, studying photovoltaics, advanced building materials, and renewable energy systems.

Right now, ISUS construction students are building replicas of six homes associated with famous Americans — Thomas Edison, John Glenn, Neil Armstrong, Amelia Earhart, Wilbur Wright, and Bessie Coleman, the first licensed African-American pilot. The six homes boast a variety of green technologies and will eventually be sold to help fund future training.

Community partnership is another hallmark of ISUS's work. The construction program's output has helped bring critical mass and additional grants to Dayton's urban renewal program by renovating thirteen boarded-up homes, overhauling an eight-unit apartment building, and constructing nearly forty new homes. In all four ISUS programs, students devote one-third of their time to community projects.

Since its inception in 1992, ISUS has garnered national attention, becoming a go-to model for programs in other states. The US Secretary of Labor, Secretary of HUD, and members of Congress have heaped accolades on the ISUS approach. In 2009, Ann was named a Purpose Prize Fellow, a prestigious award for innovative thinkers over the age of sixty whose work has advanced solutions to major social problems.

But Ann's measure of success is the changes she sees in young lives. "First, their attitudes change. Then they're willing to accept some comfort and friendship. Trust follows, and finally hope. And that's when they open up and are ready to learn and follow their dreams," she says.

As for her own long journey, Ann says, "At seventy, I'm doing exactly what I choose to do, and I don't know anything more gratifying than that. The thing that gives me joy and keeps me pushing is the difference I see in our students. Most people my age are thinking about how to live the best possible life in the winter of their years. I'm right where I want to be."

LESSONS AND INSPIRATION

YOU ARE THE AUTHOR
OF YOUR OWN STORY

Ann's life started to change the day she realized that being a victim is a choice. After she attempted to defend her mother against one of her father's rages, he stormed out the door and didn't return for two weeks. *My mother was upset with me because I ran him away,"* says Ann. *"I realized then that I could not help her with her situation. She would have to help herself."*

Today, Ann imparts the same message to her students: *"My situation wasn't one that I created as a child, but I had to play the hand I was dealt. So when I hear stories from our* students about 'Oh, my family, or my bad school, or my hard luck,' I empathize with them all. But it still always comes back to the question, 'What are you going to do with your life now?' It's all up to you."

DON'T BE HINDERED BY ANYONE ELSE'S EXPECTATIONS

Somehow, Ann learned a kind of alchemy that distilled others' low expectations of her into pure motivation — a burning desire to prove what she could do. At ISUS, she strives to give students the same experience. "We have a lot to prove, so we always ask our students to do a little more than what others believe is possible. We set a high goal, but not so high they won't believe it. If we'd told a student in the beginning what they'd be doing now, they just wouldn't have believed it," Ann says, adding, "Every year we raise the bar a little more. I'm curious to see how much higher we can raise it. We might have to extend the class by a week or two, but that's just fine. They still make the mark."

ALWAYS AIM TO EXCEL

For Ann, being the best isn't just a matter of honor or pride; it's also a solution to the lack of money and education: "Never settle for being average, or doing just enough to get by. Average is not exciting; average does not make you stand out. I've worked with some very smart people, and I found that when I invested the time to learn, I could catch up with them, even if I started behind."

A LITTLE ENCOURAGEMENT
CAN CREATE A BIG SPARK

ISUS grew partly from Ann's experience of having just one person see something in her that no one else did. Recalling how one of her teachers made a huge difference in her life without ever realizing it, she says, *"It wasn't that she knew anything about my life. She didn't heap praise on me or call attention to me. It was just that every time I walked into that class, the expression on her face said she was glad to see me, and that was a wonderful thing to know. One day, she asked me what I was going to do about college, which I hadn't really thought about. It was just an offhand remark, but she didn't ask, 'Are you going?' She said, 'How are you coming with that?' So I got busy trying to get accepted."*

TAKE THE PLUNGE,
AND YOU'LL LEARN

Throughout her life, Ann has operated with the idea that you don't learn to swim by standing at the side of the pool. *"I have always known that I can learn by doing, and I think everyone else can, too,"* she says. *"I'm not a teacher, and yet I'm creating schools. I know something about teaching people because I've had to teach my own children and I've gone through the learning experience myself. I'm not pretending to have all the answers, but I'm figuring it out. You just have to be willing to jump in and try. You have to be ready to make mistakes. If you're not making mistakes you're not being challenged enough! You just don't want those mistakes to be the same ones you made before."*

SMALL GOALS CAN
BE MEANINGFUL, TOO

"I think many people hesitate to set a goal because they think it has to be something you want to do forever. And that's not really the way it is. Goals can be incremental, requiring just simple, small steps to move you on your way. Go as far as you can see, and when you get there you can see farther."

GET CLEAR ON WHAT'S
REALLY STANDING IN YOUR WAY

"I want our students to ask, 'Are my choices moving me closer to where I want to be, or are they impeding me?' If you apply that question to every aspect of your life — your friends, the activities you choose to engage in, your work, your education — you might realize you need to change your priorities or your environment. If friends hold you back, get new friends. If relatives keep you down, make them distant relatives."

THE FABLE OF THE BOY AND HIS DOG

Ann grew up reading fables and stories, and still shares them with students to teach life lessons without preaching. One of her favorites gets across the message that we are all responsible for our own lives:

Have you heard the story about the boy and his dog?
A little boy tied his dog to the pole, but he didn't tie him

well, and while he was playing with his friends, the rope came loose and fell.

Now the dog really wanted to play, but he howled and he cried and stayed in that same spot, because he thought he was tied.

And when the boy returned and saw his dog loose and all, he patted his pet on the head and said, "You're a good dog."

But the boy, being the master, he had fun and was satisfied — and the dog could have too, but he thought he was tied.

Now, as I look at the masters and servants among men, I see the same story happening over and over, time and again. Some people are using their minds, they're creating and being satisfied.

Others — well, they're confused and crying, because they think they're tied.

S U M M I N G   U P

YOU CAN RISE ABOVE IT.

For more on Ann Higdon:

www.isusinc.com/
www.encore.org/prize/nominate?ref=candidatepage.cfm?candidateid=5745
www.youtube.com/watch?v=G_sedu8wHv4

FEARLESS

No Obstacle Too Great

COMING BACK
FROM THE DEAD

BRIAN BOYLE

Ironman Triathlete

LOOKING AT photographs of twenty-three-year-old Brian Boyle, it's obvious that he's ripped. His six-pack abs and sculpted muscles testify to the intensity and drive that lie behind his friendly, engaging manner. Then you notice the jagged scar that runs nearly the full length of his torso.

Until the age of eighteen, Brian was preoccupied with school, sports, and the immediate future, just like any other guy his age. A top-ranked competitive swimmer at his high school, he was looking forward to his freshman year at St. Mary's College in Maryland, where he already had a spot on the swim team. His other big ambition was to compete in an Ironman triathlon, a world-famous competition combining a 2.4-mile swim, a 112-mile bike ride, and a 26.2-mile run. To call the Ironman "grueling" doesn't even begin to tell it.

But life has a way of altering even the best-laid plans. Shortly after high-school graduation in 2004, as Brian was on his way home from swim practice, his car was broadsided by a dump truck. In an instant, all his hopes for the future dissolved into a pile of smoldering, jagged metal. The impact of the crash smashed his heart to the opposite side of his chest, collapsed his lungs, broke most of his ribs, clavicle, and pelvis, lacerated his liver, and caused him to lose more than 60 percent of his blood by the time he was air-lifted to the hospital on life support.

Brian was not expected to live. In fact, while in the hospital he "coded" eight times. Somehow he clung to life, finally emerging from a two-month coma to find himself strapped into a hospital bed with dozens of tubes and IVs keeping him alive. He couldn't blink, talk, or move. Having undergone fourteen operations, he was in excruciating pain.

Worse still was the gloomy prognosis laid out by the medical staff — he would never walk again; he may have suffered permanent brain damage; he would need lifelong care in a special facility. "It was like waking up in a nightmare," Brian recalls. "I couldn't believe what I was hearing. As an athlete, you're taught to never quit or give up, but every day I heard people say I had little if any chance of getting better."

Brian began to think that dying might be a relief. But then something happened that he still can't fully explain. "Even though I couldn't speak or move, my dad could sense that I was letting go," says Brian. "One day he came into my hospital room, shut the door, and just started pleading and yelling at me, telling me I had to hang on, that I could do it, that we had all come too far to give up now. I could see the fire in his eyes. Something just clicked, and in that moment I understood that I had to take charge and fight to stay alive."

Looking back, Brian describes that moment as "the passing of a baton — like a relay." Now the baton was firmly in his hands. Game on!

Over the next year he threw himself into his new full-time job: relearning how to talk, eat, walk, take a shower, tie his shoes, and dress himself. "Every day, I just did the best I could to get back to life — from a wheelchair to a walker, to a cane, to getting back on my feet, to gaining back weight, muscle, and strength, and most of all, to regaining a positive attitude," he says.

When the laborious hours of rehab left Brian drained and dispirited, he looked to others for strength. Olympic swimmer Gary Hall, one of Brian's heroes, wrote to assure him that he would one day swim again. His swim coach from St. Mary's College visited and told him the same thing. "I thought, 'If they believe in me, why not give it a try? What's to keep me from going to college and swimming competitively?'"

Defying his doctors' predictions, by the fall of 2005, a little over a year after his accident, Brian's broken body had healed to the point where he was able to register for classes at St. Mary's; he even began to train with the college swim team. But that winter, things fell apart as bouts with bronchitis, pneumonia, and mononucleosis stopped him in his tracks once again.

Frustrated, Brian turned to strength training as a way to keep advancing his recovery. He spent every spare moment in the gym, pushing himself through hours of rigorous training each day. By mid-2007, he looked more like a pro football linebacker than a swimmer. For him, it wasn't enough to survive. He wanted to prove that he was well and whole.

Out of the blue, he got an opportunity to do just that. On a whim, he had emailed an inquiry to the organizers of the world-famous Kona Ironman competition, thinking he might look toward entering it five or ten years down the road. He was floored by the response: He would be considered for one of the special inspirational slots allocated to the media and would not have to qualify based on past competitive performance. Would he like a spot in the Ironman coming up in October?

Brian wasn't naïve. It was already July, and he knew that even seasoned athletes may spend years conditioning themselves for an Ironman, honing their bodies into superbly lean and powerful human machines. At that point, weighing in at a bulked-up 230 pounds, he was in no shape to run or even jog more than a few miles, let alone compete in a triathlon.

Yet in his heart, Brian knew this was a challenge he had to take on. Doctors had told him that he'd be lucky to see his fiftieth birthday, given the damage his body had sustained. "Why wait?" he reasoned. "I had to go out there and at least attempt this thing. If I failed, then at least I'd tried."

The Ironman officials told Brian that to qualify for Kona, he would first have to get medical clearance and complete a half-Ironman, a 70-mile event that was just three weeks away. "People thought I was crazy to even consider it. But I didn't know if I would have another chance," he says. Brian put himself on a crash training regimen, rotating from pool to track to bicycle to gym for hours each day, six days a week. Whenever his energy flagged, he called up the vision of himself on life support in the ICU. He'd made it through that hell. Could a triathlon be any tougher?

The day of the race, Brian quickly fell to the back of the pack but kept himself going by thinking of all the people who'd helped him through his recovery. He kept remembering his father's voice in the ICU, saying, "We know you're in pain, but you have to keep fighting. Don't give up." It took him seven hours and thirteen minutes to complete the half-triathlon, feeling like a "walking corpse" as he crossed the finish line. But he made it, and he wasn't last, either.

Now he had some inkling of what he would be up against at Kona. No one could say how Brian's damaged organs might react to the stress of a full triathlon. With just six weeks to prepare, Brian dialed up his physical training once more while working inwardly on the total focus and mental toughness he would need. As he says, "Preparing for the Ironman is 90 percent mental and 10 percent physical."

The day of the Kona race, Brian encountered an unexpected hurdle: coping with the rush of reporters, which left him "terrified." But when one journalist asked him, "What if you *don't* finish?" Brian realized that the thought had never entered his mind. Having come so far, he had no room for doubt.

Listening as Brian recounts the Kona Ironman is like a harrowing rollercoaster ride. He vividly describes periods of total exhaustion, pain, and near-delirium alternating with moments of soaring exhilaration and renewal. Throughout, he kept going back in his mind to the vision of his parents waiting for him to surface from his coma. Now they were waiting for him at the finish line.

In October 2007, three years after his near-fatal accident, Brian once again beat the odds, completing the Kona Ironman in a little over fourteen hours and thirty minutes. "It was the best day of my life," he remembers. "When I crossed that line, it was like a second wind of life. I felt fully recovered, rejuvenated, and healed. The Ironman may have been an extreme goal, but it was my way of saying, 'We're all through with the pain, the sadness, and suffering. You don't have to worry about me anymore.'"

He hasn't let up since. In 2009, Brian competed in the Louisville, Kentucky, Ironman, where he pulled out another impressive performance, knocking four hours off his previous time. He also ran five marathons, back to back, and saw publication of his firsthand account of his astounding comeback, appropriately named *Iron Heart*. Today, he spends his time training, finishing college, and talking with others about his experience of recovery. For Brian, making the journey from dying to living has been the greatest triumph of all.

LESSONS AND INSPIRATION

LOVE CAN BE MORE POTENT THAN AMBITION

Wanting to do something for the sake of those we love is sometimes the most powerful motivator of all. In Brian's case, his concern that his parents would be devastated by his death helped fuel his will to live. *"I knew that my parents wouldn't make it without me. That was a deciding factor,"* he recalls. *"Every time I got sick, or my blood pressure rose, or my pulse started to race, I could see their fear. I wanted to show them that I was okay, that I would survive."*

TAKE SMALL STEPS TO REACH BIG GOALS

Brian's comeback demonstrates how a series of small victories can add up to a huge accomplishment: *"Each day I told myself, 'Let's see what's possible. Let's see what we can do today. Let's keep going.' That was pretty much it; I just set small goals and tried to achieve them. I didn't know at the time that each small goal would add up to something so much bigger."*

ACCEPT THE CHALLENGE AND NEVER QUIT

Bicycle crashes are a common occurrence in triathlons, and Brian knew that another accident could land him back in intensive care, maybe even kill him. But he was not about to let that stand in his way. Acknowledging that the importance of taking on risks and challenges is a timeworn cliché, Brian points out that it has a different tenor to someone who's undergone what he has. *"To survivors like myself, it means never giving up,"* he says. *"I almost gave up in the hospital and so I know how that feels. I will never do that again with anything in my life."*

GRAB OPPORTUNITY WHEN IT COMES

Brian's doctors would certainly have been happier if he'd put his Ironman dreams on hold for a while. But when the chance came, he didn't hesitate: *"The Ironman had been one of my goals for a long time. But on a deeper level, I jumped at it because I had learned you don't always get a tomorrow or a second chance. What if I wasn't around next year? It doesn't matter who you are, you never know what's around the corner."*

CLOSE THE DOOR ON NEGATIVITY

After his accident, Brian willfully shut down his doubts and fears, a strategy that aided his rapid recovery: *"I learned to just keep moving forward, to try not to dwell on the negative things and always be grateful for every second I have in life. People who have experienced extreme adversity or tragedy understand what that's all about."*

THE DARKEST MOMENTS CAN LEAD TO INSPIRATION

"I had some very rough times during recovery but would use those moments as a way to spur myself on, to just keep going, not look

back. I tried not to feel sorry for myself or bitter about what had happened. I moved from asking, 'Why did this happen to me?' to, 'What is the meaning of this and how am I going to use it?' That was my way of pulling myself through darkness and sadness."

IF YOU PUT YOUR MIND TO IT, YOU CAN DO IT

"I think most people underestimate what they can do," Brian says. And when he talks about mental strength, he's not just spouting some self-help slogan — he's speaking from his own incredible, gut-wrenching experience. "Remember that when other people say something is impossible, that's just their opinion. The Ironman slogan is, 'Anything is possible,' and I truly believe it. I think it really comes down to a positive mindset. Go out there, set the goal, and be determined to achieve it. If you put your mind to something, you can do great things."

S U M M I N G   U P

IF YOU'VE GOT THE INSPIRATION AND THE WILL,
THERE'S NOTHING YOU CAN'T DO.

For more on Brian Boyle:

Boyle, Brian, and Katovsky, Bill. *Iron Heart: The True Story of How I Came Back from the Dead.* New York: Skyhorse Publishing, 2009.

http://brianboyle.wordpress.com/

THE SACRIFICE
FOR JUSTICE

CARLOTTA WALLS LANIER
Civil Rights Pioneer

THINK OF the civil rights movement, and chances are you'll think of Martin Luther King, Jr., intoning "I have a dream" from the steps of the Lincoln Memorial as a crowd of 200,000 roared back the cry for freedom.

But the fiercest battles for civil rights weren't fought in Washington, D.C. They were fought in the day-to-day lives of ordinary people with no crowds to cheer them on. The course of history was changed in Alabama, when Rosa Parks refused to give up her seat on a bus. In North Carolina, by four young black students who sat down at a Woolworth's lunch counter. And in Arkansas, when a group of teenagers who became known as the Little Rock Nine walked through the doors of the all-white Central High School.

The youngest of the Little Rock Nine was Carlotta Walls, a tall, soft-spoken fourteen-year-old whose parents had instilled in her the idea that a good education is the key to a good life. Carlotta had always wanted to do well in school, competing for high marks with the other serious students at the segregated schools she attended.

It was 1957 when the Little Rock school board finally, reluctantly, agreed to racially integrate its schools as ordered under the historic *Brown v. Board of Education* Supreme Court decision three years earlier. Carlotta was one of the first black students to enroll at Central High. But in recounting the tumultuous events of that time, she explains that she never intended her brave action to be a political statement. Her goal was simply to get the best education she could. Central High was one of the top forty high schools in the country, and it was less than a mile from Carlotta's home.

Raised with good Southern manners, Carlotta had been taught to treat adults with respect and speak only when spoken to. The last thing she wanted was to become a national symbol of the battle for school desegregation. "Many people believed that we wanted to go to Central High for our race, but that was never the motivating factor," she says. "It was about getting the same thing that white people were getting, like better books.

It was about having access to the same opportunities, not about sitting next to a white person."

Now that the doors of Central High had been forced open to her, Carlotta was ready to prove herself. "You just don't know what that does for a person, when a law can no longer be used against you," she says. "I always knew that I was just as good as anyone else. Now the law said I was right and anybody who wanted to keep me out of school was wrong."

But as the Little Rock Nine were all well aware, the vast majority of Central High families didn't want them there. The NAACP had briefed the students, advising them to avoid all contact with protestors. School officials privately told them that they would be strictly monitored and, to avoid further inflaming the situation, would not be allowed to participate in school sports, dances, or other extracurricular activities. Everyone expected to see protestors outside Central High for a few days or weeks. No one anticipated the escalating hatred and violence that would put Central High School on the front lines of the national battle for school integration.

On the first day of school, Carlotta woke up excited to be starting senior high and put on a new dress for the occasion. She and the other black students walked together toward the high school, surrounded by a phalanx of ministers. They could hear the crowd long before they saw it. As Carlotta clutched her books to her chest and looked straight ahead, a sea of angry faces came into view. It seemed to rise from all sides, spitting at them and hurling racial insults as the black students approached the school. "There must have been hundreds of people ... faces contorted ... pumping their fists in the air and shouting … children waving Confederate flags and mimicking their parents. Just who were these people?" Carlotta later wrote in her memoir, *A Mighty Long Way*. "Their words sounded muddled except for one: nigger … nigger … nigger."

Carlotta kept walking, straight and tall, aware that she was representing not just herself but also her family and community. She refused to acknowledge or respond to the venom that surrounded her. In her book, she recalls thinking, "Do not stoop to their level. You are a Walls. Just take the next step, and the next."

The beleaguered group finally reached the edge of the school grounds, only to be turned away. Citing the potential for violence, the Arkansas governor had called in the National Guard to block the entrance to the school. It took three weeks of fierce legal wrangling before the Little Rock Nine were finally allowed into Central High. That happened on September 25, 1957, and then only because an angry President Dwight D. Eisenhower had insisted that the law be upheld, sending the 101st Airborne Division to escort the black students inside.

The 1957–58 school year proved to be the worst of Carlotta's life. Each of the Little Rock Nine would pay an enormous personal price for breaking the color barrier at Central High. Carlotta's good friend, Minnie, was expelled for retaliating in anger to relentless harassment in January 1958. Five other black students left the school after Governor Orval Faubus closed all the high schools in Little Rock. Carlotta was one of only three out of the original nine who stayed on at Central High to graduate.

Those who stuck it out endured an ongoing, daily barrage of harassment, despite the armed troops escorting them to their classes. In the hallways, they ran a gauntlet of racial slurs, trying to avoid large gobs of spit that seemed to fly at them out of nowhere. Carlotta learned to wipe her face off without turning to look for the perpetrator. The black students were pushed, tripped, shoved, and kicked from behind when they stooped to pick up the books that had been knocked from their arms. The cafeteria, where food was thrown along with taunts, was the worst.

Thrown headlong into this hostile environment, Carlotta quickly learned that she had to shut down her emotions in order to survive. "I was trying to be the strong person that I was already developing into before Central High, and not allow my heart to get into it," she recalls. "But sometimes I would let my guard down." On many days she was so emotionally depleted that she was unable to do her homework.

Yet, true to her deeply pragmatic nature, Carlotta found practical ways to cope with life at Central High. "You look at a problem, decide on the solution, and work toward it; I learned that early," she says. Rather than brave the lunch line, she brought her lunch every day and sat with her back against the wall, where she could monitor her surroundings. She held her head high and refused to allow eye contact with her persecutors, knowing that any wrong move might get her expelled. When, astonishingly, the Arkansas governor buckled under segregationist pressure and closed all local high schools for a full year, Carlotta continued to earn high-school credits by taking correspondence courses, attending summer school, and moving in with families in other school districts.

Carlotta's best defense was a strong mental attitude that helped her stave off self-doubt. "I was reminded daily that what doesn't kill you makes you stronger," she relates. "I always did think, 'If they don't see that I'm just as good as they are, it is their problem, not mine.' That was just their ignorance speaking." Her matter-of-fact attitude also helped spare her the bitter disappointment she saw in some friends who had expected the tide of racial hatred to recede at Central High. "I wasn't about to expend good energy after bad to change closed minds," she says. "You accept what is, and know that this too shall pass."

What did pierce Carlotta's mental armor was one terrifying act of violence. One rainy night, while her father was at work and the rest of the family slept, a bomb shattered the front window of Carlotta's home. To the family's horror, her father was named a suspect in the case. Even though he was never charged, his questioning by the police stirred new fear among the black families in the community. A friend of Carlotta's was later jailed for the crime, though she and many others knew that he was innocent.

"My actions had brought this to our home and neighborhood, and it took a very long time to reconcile with that," says Carlotta. "I felt guilty even though I knew that everything I had done was for good. All the same, it was such a terrible sacrifice for my family."

But no threat, however serious, was going to keep Carlotta from graduating, an event that was just months away. Her parents had always taught Carlotta to finish what she started, no matter what the personal cost. "I couldn't think of quitting, because I would be quitting not just on myself but on others," she says. "Quitting is not part of my DNA."

On May 30, 1960, a nervous Carlotta Walls walked quickly across the stage at Central High School to receive her diploma. She shudders at the thought that she could have been denied this accomplishment. "I needed that diploma to validate all the things I had gone through," she explains. "If I hadn't had something to show for it ... how devastating that would be."

Though she didn't fully realize it at the time, Carlotta set an example for countless others by putting fear aside and taking enormous risks to reach her goal. She sacrificed every semblance of a normal high school experience for one simple principle: A young black woman is entitled to the same education as her white counterparts.

With graduation, the worst days of her life were over, and she left Little Rock immediately afterwards. But the price Carlotta paid for her accomplishment was exacted over many years. She never went back to her hometown except for funerals and the briefest of visits. Though she started college at the first opportunity, she had trouble concentrating — a problem that today might be attributed to post-traumatic stress. It took several years before Carlotta was able to settle down and begin working in earnest toward her college degree. She went on to a successful college and business career, founding her own real estate brokerage firm, LaNier and Company, which she still operates with her son, Whitney. She is also active in her community and is president of the Little Rock Nine Foundation.

For thirty years, Carlotta wouldn't talk about Central High School to anyone but close family. She could hardly bear the memories. But when members of the Little Rock Nine were awarded the Congressional Gold Medal in 1999, her story was finally revealed. Many of her friends were astounded that they had not known Carlotta's place in history.

On the 40th anniversary of the year that the Little Rock Nine entered Central High School, the group was invited back for a grand celebration with dozens of dignitaries. Once again, a loud crowd gathered at the school, but this time their greeting was jubilant. Carlotta remembers the next part well: There, holding open the doors to the high school, were President Bill Clinton and Arkansas Governor Mike Huckabee. The Little Rock Nine walked through proudly, heads held high.

LESSONS AND INSPIRATION

THINK OF YOUR TOUGHEST CHALLENGES AS A JOB TO GET DONE

Most of her group's nine original members left Central High, and Carlotta herself could have transferred to public and private schools in more tolerant states. But that would have been giving in. To keep defeat at bay, Carlotta changed the way she thought about school. *"Early on, I started to think of school as my job,"* she recalls. *"When you have a job, you wake up in the morning, eat breakfast, get dressed, and then go to work. You don't think, 'Well, do I want to do this today or not?' You go to your job whether you like it or not. And then you come home and start over again the next day. You don't quit."*

THE POSSIBILITIES FOR CHANGE
MAY BE GREATER THAN YOU THINK

Not until a family trip to New York before high school did Carlotta have the chance to see people of all colors living side by side without fear or stigma. As she remembers, *"My parents had always told me I was as good as anyone else, and in New York, I saw that freedom to be just who I was. That freedom said to me, 'This is the way it can be.' So when I came back to Little Rock, I knew that the attitudes there weren't because of me. I didn't take it all that personally. I understood that it was just that the laws were wrong, and those were going to change."*

CHOOSE ROLE MODELS
WHOSE PATHS YOU CAN FOLLOW

Carlotta drew inspiration from many role models, including her hero, Jackie Robinson, who broke the color barrier in baseball, and Rosa Parks, who ignited a movement for freedom by refusing to give up her seat on a bus. But then there was Emmett Till, the boy in Mississippi who was murdered for allegedly whistling at a white woman. *"I was always very aware of the consequences of my choices, and the consequences that others had faced before me,"* says Carlotta. *"I had all these role models — good, bad, or indifferent — and they all followed different paths. You have to decide which path you want to go down."*

THERE'S MORE THAN ONE WAY
TO BE A TRAILBLAZER

Private and quiet, Carlotta proves that you don't have to be an outspoken activist to change the world. She was always the one in the background when the press wanted to talk with the Little Rock Nine, and yet her impact was equal to theirs. *"We were nine students with nine stories, none greater or lesser than the other. We all had our own way of doing things,"* she says, pointing out that even later in life, she didn't participate in any of the civil rights marches. *"I am not one to go around with a banner. I believe that actions speak louder than words; that's just who I am."*

PICK YOUR BATTLES CAREFULLY,
AND FIGHT TO WIN

Carlotta understood that she didn't have the emotional energy to change minds, and that it might not be possible to combat the ignorance, hatred, and bigotry that surrounded her. *"Not every battle is worth taking on, and some take more energy than they are worth. I might see things that are wrong but I'm not going to work hard for change unless it is a win/win situation,"* she says. She chose to direct her energy toward graduating, never questioning that this was the right battle to fight and win.

STAY FOCUSED ON
WHAT'S MOST IMPORTANT TO YOU

Through all the anguish of her high school years, Carlotta never lost sight of the personal goal that had brought her to Central High — to get the best possible education: *"All my life I've wanted to put my energy into something that gives me a good result. At Central High, my goal was to learn, do well in classes, and graduate. That was why I was there."*

CARLOTTA'S ADVICE TO STUDENTS

- Never forget that you are just as good as the next person.
- Be willing to take risks for what you believe in.
- Make decisions based on what you know is best for you, not on what your peers tell you.
- Stand up to bullies and be accountable for yourself and your friends.
- Don't take on everything that comes along; save your energy for your greatest goals.
- Learn US history for a deeper appreciation of the opportunities you now have.

SUMMING UP

WHEN YOU ARE CLEAR ON

WHAT YOU CAN DO —

AND INTEND TO DO —

NO ONE CAN KEEP YOU DOWN.

For more on Carlotta Walls LaNier:

LaNier, Carlotta Walls, and Page, Lisa Frazier. *A Mighty Long Way: My Journey to Justice at Little Rock Central High School.* New York: One World/Ballantine, 2009.

www.littlerock9.com
www.encyclopediaofarkansas.net

LEAVING DISADVANTAGE
AND DISABILITY BEHIND

JULIA K. ANDERSON
Blind Alpine Ski Racer

A PRETTY WOMAN with dark eyes and porcelain skin, Julia Anderson greets you from a black wheelchair that seems to swallow her small frame. Attached to the chair is a respirator connected to tubing that helps her breathe. It's a sight that inspires sympathy. But Julia is anything but self-pitying, despite the catalog of troubles and suffering she has endured.

Until she was four, Julia lived in the eastern bloc of Central Europe in a volatile family situation. When Julia's mother could no longer tolerate the abuse of her alcoholic husband, she fled to the United States, taking Julia and her sister with her. They settled in a West Coast suburb. Julia began to fall ill near the end of fifth grade, and when her weight dropped to 50 pounds she was diagnosed with juvenile diabetes. At home, Julia was often caught in the fallout of her mother's stressful adjustment to a new life. Julia doesn't blame her mother, pointing out that "abuse leads to abuse." But she reached a breaking point and ran away several times before permanently entering the foster care system in seventh grade. Bounced from home to home, she spent the next six years feeling lonely and isolated.

In high school, Julia began to notice changes in her vision. Some days she could see, but on many days the shapes in front of the classroom were a blur. By the age of sixteen she was legally blind. Without a family to lean on, Julia recalls, "I was extremely frightened. I could not imagine life without color, without the ability to look in a mirror, without true independence. I wondered how I would get through the day alone. I wondered if I could ever learn Braille and how I was going to get through college." She had already attended two high schools as she was moved around in the foster care system and was now transferred to a third high school that offered easier access to services for the visually impaired.

One day Julia joined a school ski trip to the mountains sponsored by the Foundation for the Junior Blind in Los Angeles. She wasn't an athlete and she wasn't particularly interested in skiing, but peer pressure made her go. With a guide as a lead, her first trip down the slopes was sheer terror. But by the end of the day, her terror had changed to exhilaration and the most perfect sense of joy she had ever felt. "Skiing was total freedom for me," she says. "It did not connect to anything else I had ever done. It was an experience of living totally in the moment and responding completely to the terrain. I fell in love."

Julia had no money, no equipment, and no training, but once she discovered her passion she wanted to perfect it. She went to the mountains with the Foundation whenever she could. She learned to trust her guides and to follow what they asked her to do. When bystanders told her she should consider professional racing, she enlisted the help of an instructor and began to tackle steeper and more dangerous ski runs.

Julia had a gift for speed. "I began to live by a new standard, a new rule: 'I will try anything once, and if it doesn't kill me I will try it again.' I was eager to open my life to new experiences," she says. And try she did, eventually reaching speeds of 50 to 60 miles per hour down the steepest slopes. To the surprise of many, she qualified to compete in the US national championships after one hectic marathon that took her to back-to-back races in Lake Tahoe and Colorado.

Now came the hard part: finding the money for travel, fees, clothing, and equipment that included four or five pairs of professional-level skis. The summer after she turned seventeen, Julia wrote more than 300 letters to companies she hoped would sponsor her quest to become a world-class skier. Her goal was simple: train, compete with the US national team, and win as many medals as she could.

"It's not going to work," people told her. "You shouldn't

even try. You'll just be disappointed." Julia understood that her goal seemed impossible to most people, but to her it was achievable. "I have never listened to what other people tell me I can and can't do," she says. "How can anyone else decide that for you? You're the only one who can decide what you're capable of doing."

One of her 300 letters found its mark, and Julia won the support of a sponsor. For the next eight years, she lived her dream, competing as a semi-professional alpine ski racer. She qualified for the national championships in the "visually-impaired" categories every year, competing in international events in the United States and around the world. Julia was a "four tracker," meaning she had skis attached both to her poles and her feet when she raced. "I had more hardware on me than the entire US team combined," she jokes. To supplement her income, she became a professional speaker and spoke to the United Way, the Foundation for the Junior Blind, and many other groups. She sought out schoolchildren and teens, particularly those in foster care, and shared her own story about overcoming obstacles and not fitting in.

In one race, while being filmed for a segment on TV, Julia fell near the finish line and suffered a severe fracture. Later, in her hospital bed, she considered for the first time giving up racing in the speed events. "But after the initial thought went through my mind, it exited just as quickly. My next thought was, 'I want to go harder and faster,'" she says.

Julia's fall signaled that she was becoming increasingly ill. For years her symptoms had been attributed to diabetes, but she had always known that wasn't correct. In fact, her failing eyesight and muscle weakness stemmed from a far more serious disease, a rare form of multiple sclerosis called Devic's syndrome. Devic's is characterized by optic nerve and spinal cord swelling, the sudden onset of vision loss, and weakness in the lower and upper extremities that frequently leads to permanent confinement to a wheelchair.

Devic's syndrome is incurable and progressive, and yet the diagnosis brought Julia some comfort after years of not knowing what was wrong. By now she had her own apartment and was in college, and her hard-won independence was threatened by deteriorating health. She began to experience violent nausea and vomiting whenever she lay down and tried to sleep. Because this happened primarily at night, Julia began to dread the approach of darkness. She tried to sit up and stay awake, but whenever her head would droop the nausea would start all over again. In the morning she was generally able to rest for a few hours before attending her classes, which she carefully scheduled for the afternoons.

Doctors were unable to alleviate her symptoms, and a desperate Julia began to believe that death would be a welcome relief from her daily suffering. She voluntarily entered hospice care, putting herself in the hands of people who could tend to her through the last days of her life. She stopped eating and drinking. Fewer than 10 percent of people entering hospice care live longer than a year, but once again Julia defied the odds. She discovered new strengths in herself, and by persevering in her own research, she found medication that relieved her nausea. After seven months she left hospice, determined to live as full a life as possible.

Julia's rare disease brought her into contact with Vivian, a fellow Devic's-sufferer who became her greatest friend and hero. "Vivian faced Devic's with unrelenting courage, and she gave me a purpose by allowing me to help her for a decade until she passed away," says Julia. "It was a priceless gift — to make me think, to make me eager, to make me creative in trying to meet her needs. I thrived on her remarkable, courageous spirit. The joy she brought me was immeasurable!"

Today, at thirty-seven, Julia is as full of resolve as ever. Devic's has taken its toll on her body, but not on her steel-willed spirit. She's working on a book. She goes on outings with friends. She insists on living on her own, accepting only a modest amount of care as she fiercely protects her independence. Julia knows that her life has not followed a normal trajectory, but she is also aware that she has pushed through limits that few people can even imagine.

And skiing? It's still in the picture. Last winter, Julia enlisted friends to take her to the mountains. The gear took a long time to get on and her friends insisted on safety measures that frustrated her. But then she finally boarded the ski lift up the mountain. Off came the respirator and then Julia was once again flying down the slopes at full throttle. It wasn't long before she talked the ski patrol into taking her to the dangerous runs at higher elevations, leaving her friends far below.

LESSONS AND INSPIRATION

DON'T LET NEGATIVE EMOTIONS
RULE YOUR LIFE

Julia allows herself to grieve for things she cannot change, including her declining health and the loss of her friend Vivian. But she refuses to sink into depression and has even developed her own method of working through dark periods. Her secret? *"I give myself a limit when I feel down, because otherwise it's easy to get stuck. Sometimes I give myself a day, or maybe even a week. I'll even mark each day off the calendar — okay, one more day to feel sad. When I get to my limit, I move on with my life. I've learned to stop the negative before it turns into a mountain."*

SET A GOAL AND
BE WILLING TO PAY THE PRICE

"I was absolutely willing to do whatever it took to become a sponsored racer. I spent an entire summer in my room, writing 300 personalized letters. I had no idea who would respond, but I was certain that someone would, because I had made a decision to be successful."

NEGATIVES CAN BE
TURNED INTO POSITIVES

It all depends on your mindset, Julia believes: *"When I think about the past, I see that what might have been negative at the time turned out well in the end. Certain things had to happen for me* to know what I know and be who I am today. If you look at life that way, you see that what you have learned every step of the way is going to help you for the rest of your life."

SOMEHOW, THE RIGHT
PEOPLE SHOW UP
WHEN YOU NEED THEM

Whether you call it luck or call it faith, Julia's experience has taught her that she's not alone. Good people are out there and ready to help. *"I am who I am because of the amazing people who have always shown up in my life at exactly the right time, giving me the support and encouragement I need,"* she says. *"It was like that when I needed a ski sponsor, when I needed spiritual support, when I needed a good neurologist, and when I needed a friend. These extraordinary, wonderful people are there for us all; they are angels on earth."*

LIMITS FADE WHEN
YOU CONFRONT THEM

"I used to think if 'A' happened I wouldn't want to live, or if 'B' happened I wouldn't want to live. But it changes when you get there. The limit you imagined is not really your limit once you are facing it. You see that it's not so bad after all, that you can get through the worst you could imagine. If someone told me my life story as if it were someone else, I would say get out of here! No way could I ever do that! But I did, and I can."

SUMMING UP

THE LIMITS YOU IMAGINE ARE NOT REAL;
YOU CAN ENDURE AND ACCOMPLISH
MUCH MORE THAN YOU THINK.

Author's Note: "Julia K. Anderson" is the pseudonym of a real person who wishes to tell her story while maintaining her privacy because of issues surrounding her health.

RESILIENT

Lives Reinvented

FROM LOSER
TO LEADER

SCOTT H. SILVERMAN

Founder and Executive Director,
Second Chance

THE STORY of Scott Silverman is proof that failure can be the springboard to a life of purpose and meaning. Through his school years, he was a poster child for attitude and disciplinary problems. Today he runs an award-winning program that turns lives around.

Scott was labeled a rebel almost as soon as he started school. Bad things just seemed to happen to him. In second grade, a classmate threw a shoe at him on the playground. Scott threw it back and broke the child's leg. He was transferred to a different school, the first of many such moves triggered by his behavior. "My second or third week there, I was asked to point to the Atlantic Ocean on a map," he recalls. "I knew I had a fifty-fifty chance of getting it right. I got it wrong and the whole class laughed at me. I was filled with shame and promised myself that nothing like that would ever happen again. That's the day I got my Green Beret hat, put on my camouflage, and went to war."

Today Scott's discipline and learning problems might be diagnosed as ADHD, but when he was growing up, there was no such label explaining his inability to concentrate and his poor academic performance. He believed he was a failure, stupid, and unable to succeed, and he had plenty of negative reinforcement from his peers. He fought back by becoming a master of disruption in the classroom. It got so bad that in fifth grade, he was blamed for giving his teacher a heart attack.

As Scott's resistance to authority deepened, so did his desire to escape his anger and frustration. By the time he finished high school, he was anesthetizing himself with drugs and alcohol, stealing to support his habit.

In the years after graduation, Scott married and worked full-time in his family's business. He put in long days, but they were followed by long nights blurred by alcohol, cocaine, and pot. People knew he had a problem, but few knew how severe it really was. Scott often blacked out and would wake up unable to remember what he had done the night before. But when his wife handed him the phone and a list of people to call with apologies, he knew it wasn't good.

It all came to a head on a business trip to New York. Scott got into a bar brawl and was hauled back to his hotel by the police. For the first time, he felt powerless to conceal the truth about himself. "I had been hiding my thoughts, feelings, and dreams all my life," he says. "The hiding led to more drug use, more self-hatred, and more hiding. I couldn't keep doing it." The next morning he found himself alone in a coworker's office on the forty-fourth floor of a skyscraper. The window was open. He leaned over the ledge and felt the cold air on his skin. Just as he was getting ready to jump, the door opened and his associate burst in, yelling, "Get away from that window before you fall!" In that moment, Scott says, "Something happened in me that felt like divine intervention. I flew home that night and enrolled in rehab the next day."

As he completed rehab, Scott heard a piece of advice that has carried him through the years: "To keep it alive, give it away." He became an avid and intensely dedicated volunteer, putting in thousands of hours at a residential treatment center and a community food program. He saw the same prison parolees, homeless street people, and chronic drug abusers at both places — people tagged as losers, just as he had been. He knew all about self-perpetuating cycles of failure. He also saw how little the social service system seemed able to help. Scott thought he could do better with a radically different approach — one empowering and challenging the down-and-out to help themselves.

In 1993, Scott opened the doors to Second Chance, an intensive program that works to break the cycles of unemployment, homelessness, substance abuse, and crime. Instead of propping people up, the program focuses on changing negative attitudes and stripping away the armor of resentment and anger that feeds destructive behaviors. Scott couldn't have imagined the success that would follow: To date, Second Chance has served over 100,000 people, thousands of whom have gone on to lead productive lives. In 2008, he gained national recognition as a CNN "Hero."

It has been twenty-five years since Scott made the decision to live a clean and sober life. He still marks the day each November when he chose to take off the camouflage and stop hiding. When he did that, he gave himself a second chance at life. Now his calling, as he sees it, is to pass that chance along to others.

LESSONS AND INSPIRATION

TO CHANGE YOUR LIFE,
CHANGE YOUR ATTITUDE

One of the first exercises in the Second Chance training is an introduction to Scott Silverman. It seems simple enough: Hold yourself erect, look him in the eye, and shake his hand. It turns out that he isn't assessing your clothes or your hair, but your attitude. *"No matter how smart you are or how many degrees you hold, if you have a bad attitude it will be apparent and you will sabotage your success. You will close doors and eliminate opportunities for yourself. You will make people resentful and angry,"* he says. *"You can't change other people's attitudes toward you, but you can change yours toward them. To me, if that is the only tool you have, you can do great things."*

THE TRUTH WILL SET YOU FREE

"When you see the objective truth — not your story, not my story, but the facts about what got you to where you are right now — you begin to open up to how you feel about that," Scott says. *"That's when things can begin to change."*

SHARE YOUR STRENGTHS

Few people talk as passionately as Scott about the benefits of service. He recommends it not just for altruistic reasons but also because it offers insight into our own strengths and needs. *"Recovery opened my desire to serve others and to give back. There are so many people in desolate situations who need help. I still volunteer about fifteen hours a week. It's my gift to myself, and it keeps me sane. It's a way to share experience, strength, and hope, and I find that there is something I can relate to in every person I meet. It keeps my heart full."*

ASK FOR HELP WHEN YOU NEED IT

Scott has learned from years of experience that the people who need help the most are often the least likely to ask for it.

"If you ask for assistance, you might not get it, but if you don't ask, you will definitely not get it," he says. *"So ask, and ask again. Things go wrong all the time — you lose your job, your home, your car. Maybe you've played by the rules but things still fail. When you've done the best you can, put up your hand and ask for help. Don't let your pride get in the way. The world is filled with people who might help if only they knew."*

TAKE STOCK
OF YOUR TOOLBOX

"If you have a toolbox that you carry through life, you don't have to start all over again whenever you make mistakes. You just fix it," Scott says.

His list of essential tools for life includes:

- **Attitude:** *"We ask everyone who walks into Second Chance to adopt a great attitude, and we practice it ourselves. Attitude does not just happen; it can be taught."*

- **Truth:** *"Human dignity is enhanced and preserved when we are able to talk about indisputable facts and identify the problems to be solved."*

- **Integrity:** *"Integrity is who you are and what you do when no one is watching. You're the only one you have to live with for the rest of your life."*

S U M M I N G   U P

DON'T EVER BELIEVE YOU'RE NO GOOD;

YOU CAN CHANGE YOUR LIFE,

STARTING WITH

YOUR OWN ATTITUDE.

For more on Scott H. Silverman:

Silverman, Scott. *Tell Me No. I Dare You!* Tennessee: GKS Books, 2010.

www.scotthsilverman.com
www.secondchanceprogram.org/
www.cnn.com/SPECIALS/cnn.heroes/archive/scott.silverman.html

FAILURE IS NOT AN OPTION

JERRY ACUFF

Founder and CEO, Delta Point

FROM THE MOMENT you shake his hand, Jerry Acuff exudes confidence, charisma, and a can-do attitude. With his ready humor and well-honed listening skills, he's the kind of person you might describe as a born salesman. But listen to his story, and you'll discover that he's every inch the self-made man — someone who spent years forging business success from the shards of broken dreams and hard times.

Today, Jerry is a nationally recognized sales guru who runs his own multi-million-dollar consulting firm, which trains sales and marketing teams for a blue-chip list of pharmaceutical companies and other Fortune 500 clients. He is the author of three acclaimed books on sales and business leadership, frequently speaks at high-profile business events, and has been to the White House to share his views on healthcare reform.

Yet early in life, Jerry had few goals beyond survival. As he was growing up, his parents divorced "nine times between the two of them," he says. Money, or rather the lack of it, was a perpetual problem. His father filed for bankruptcy three times, and Jerry recalls coming home to a dark house because the electric bill hadn't been paid. The experience had a lasting impact. "I've never been motivated by wanting a lot of money; I've always been motivated by the fear of having no money at all," he explains.

For a time, it looked like football might be his ticket to success. Jerry was a first-team all-state football player in Florida, which earned him a scholarship to the Virginia Military Institute. He wanted to be a college football coach after graduation, but the door to that career slammed shut when his application to graduate school was rejected. "I figured nobody gets rejected by Northeast Louisiana University, but somehow I managed," he says wryly. "I was not a good student."

Jerry next tried a stint at sales but found he was terrible at it. He would often sit in his car for an hour or more, frozen with fear, before summoning the nerve to call on a client. He tried applying to law school but was wait-listed.

Desperate to make a living any way he could, Jerry turned back to sales. "I mistakenly thought anyone can sell, even though I'd previously failed at it," he says. "I had a lot to learn."

Jerry managed to get hired as a sales representative for Hoechst Pharmaceuticals and threw himself into his work with newfound intensity. When he was promoted to district manager, a job that involved teaching others how to sell, he decided it was time to work seriously on building his skills and motivation. The first book he picked up, by football legend Roger Staubach, had a quote that hit him right between the eyes: *You will be the same person in five years as you are today, except for the people you meet and the books you read.*

For the first time, Jerry understood that his career potential was directly related to how much learning he poured into himself. He began to read everything he could get his hands on about selling, management, motivation, and goal-setting. He listened to books on tape every time he got in his car. "I drove a lot, and in three years I got a second college education," he says. From a self-described "dumb jock," Jerry Acuff grew into a top-tier sales executive and coach.

When Jerry decided to start his own sales consulting business in 1995, he thought it would be relatively easy. Instead, his move into the world of start-ups was a jarring wake-up call. Four years later he was back to square one, with no savings and $100,000 in credit card debt. It was all he could do to make the minimum monthly payments.

To most people, carrying a six-figure credit card balance spells financial failure — but not to Jerry. He was determined to succeed as an entrepreneur and knew his capabilities well enough to believe he could do it. If there was one thing he had learned along the way, it was to be very clear about his goals. "A goal is not what you wish or hope for, but what you intend to achieve. When you have that clarity, you can assess whether what you're attempting is truly possible or not," says Jerry.

"Succeeding in my own business became my life's challenge. Maybe things weren't going to happen in the time-frame I wanted. Maybe I was a slow learner, or overestimated my own value, or thought I was smarter than I was. None of that mattered. I was not going to quit. Failure was not an option."

Armed with the lessons from his earlier missteps, Jerry and his wife, Maryann, steadily built their consulting business year by year, and sold the company in 2001. Soon Jerry launched another consulting business, starting all over again with just a single client. Today, Delta Point is a thriving concern that ranks among the top sales consulting firms in the country.

Still a voracious reader, Jerry keeps track of the titles he has devoured: 511 business books, and counting. And he still thinks about failure, just not in the same way. "Once you get past the fear that you will fail," he says, "you start to ask, 'What am I really capable of doing? How much further can I go? What can I do with this life?'" Jerry knows one thing for certain: It's all up to him — and it always has been.

LESSONS AND INSPIRATION

SUCCESS COMES
AT A PRICE

"I don't know anyone who is wildly successful who hasn't worked really hard and faced a lot of adversity along the way," Jerry says. *"There's a false sense that success can come to us easily, that we shouldn't have to try so hard. I'm here to tell you that's not true."*

LISTEN TO PEOPLE
WHO CAN HELP YOU SEE
YOUR OWN POTENTIAL

At one point Jerry ran into a former business partner who asked how he was doing. *"When I told him how much I was making, he said, 'Is that all? With the kind of value you're delivering, you should be making a million a year.' I began to believe he was right."* At a crucial point, Jerry's resolve was strengthened by the potential that someone else saw in him.

Jerry believes that we all have the potential for great accomplishments, but it's easy to be blindsided by perceptions of our own limitations: *"We often talk ourselves out of trying because we don't have the vision or foresight to know what we can do with our own capabilities. Find someone who believes in you, whether it's a boss or a friend, and then listen and learn from what they have to say. And act on that advice!"*

STRONG RELATIONSHIPS
ARE THE KEY TO SUCCESS

Studies show that even in this era of web-based job hunting, two out of three positions are still filled through networking. As Jerry points out, this argues for putting energy into building and maintaining good relationships at every stage of your career. *"I constantly seek people with wisdom and insight to bring into my own personal network,"* he says. *"I do a lot of relationship-building, not because I'm a big extrovert, but because I know that the wider my network is and the more people I've created value for, the more likely I am to be successful myself."*

BE CRYSTAL CLEAR ABOUT
WHAT YOU WANT TO ACHIEVE

Jerry believes that most people who fail do so because they never have real clarity about what they want in life: *"People have lots of dreams, wishes, and desires, but they never truly focus on their goals and whether they can realistically achieve them. When you have clear goals, you can weigh the pros and cons of every decision without getting tied up in what other people think. But you can only achieve your goals if you know what they are."*

FEAR OF FAILURE
CAN BE A POWERFUL MOTIVATOR

Once Jerry got into the business world, he was driven in large part by his refusal to settle for the hand-to-mouth way of life he'd experienced growing up. *"For me, part of continued success is never losing that fear of failure,"* he says. *"Only today, it's not about me, but my clients. I never want to let them down."*

WHEN YOU HAVE GOOD BOSSES, FOLLOW THEIR LEAD

"A lot of people don't win the boss lottery, but I certainly did. The first three bosses I had were some of the greatest people in the world, not to mention great teachers. They knew how to encourage people and how to build them up. After I watched them in action for fourteen years, it became part of my own style. So much of my success I attribute to the people who shaped me when I was shapable."

JERRY'S THREE RULES OF SUCCESS

These are the hard-won lessons that Jerry has woven into his sales methods and training:

1   **If it's to be, it's up to me.** *"No matter how much guidance or support we have, we are the ones who make the personal decision to reach a goal or change our lives; no one else can do that for us. The engine that drives self-development is self-awareness."*

2   **Success and failure are never final unless you let them be.** *"Just two things keep people from being successful: a lack of understanding about how to think about the events and obstacles that happen in life, and the unwillingness to go the extra mile."*

3 **Success is always a byproduct of doing the right thing.**
"True success is not measured by money, power, or position. Success is the balance between giving and receiving. In my personal life, I want to be a good steward of the resources I have and use them to help others achieve more. And in my business life, I will always go the extra mile to do the right thing for a client, because it comes back to me. It's one of the laws of the universe: When you give, you get."

S U M M I N G U P

WHAT YOU'RE CAPABLE OF

DEPENDS TOTALLY

ON YOUR COMMITMENT

TO LEARNING AND HARD WORK.

For more on Jerry Acuff:

Acuff, Jerry, and Wood, Wally. *Stop Acting Like a Seller and Start Thinking Like a Buyer.* Hoboken: Wiley, 2007.

Acuff, Jerry, and Wood, Wally. *The Relationship Edge: The Key to Strategic Influence and Selling Success.* Hoboken: Wiley, 2006.

Acuff, Jerry, and Wood, Wally. *The Relationship Edge in Business: Connecting with Customers and Colleagues When It Counts.* Hoboken: Wiley, 2004.

www.gottochange.com

SCHOOLED IN THE STREETS

Francisco Reveles

*Educational Troubleshooter
and Gang Mediator*

WHO WANTS TO join me up here?" Francisco Reveles asks his audience of nearly 1,500 high school students, including rival gang-bangers, teenage moms, and soon-to-be dropouts. As he surveys the crowd in this heavily Latino high school, one lone girl raises her hand. Francisco nods, and she walks nervously to the stage as the other students point and giggle, erupting into laughter when she stumbles. By the time she reaches Francisco at center stage, she's soaked in sweat and beet-red with embarrassment.

"What do you want to be when you finish school?" he asks. "A doctor," she answers hesitantly. The crowd hoots again, then lapses into stunned silence as Francisco thanks her and hands her a crisp $100 bill. The girl grins as she walks triumphantly back to her seat.

"Who wants to come up now?" Francisco asks. Hundreds of hands shoot up. "Too bad," he says with a theatrical shrug. "You had the opportunity and passed it up. Life is hard, *mijos.* You've got to grab your chance when it comes around." The point hits home. Francisco knows how to reach even the toughest kids because he, too, came from the tough streets of the barrio. He might easily have become yet another dropout statistic, as an estimated four in ten Latino males in America are today. He might even have ended up behind bars, or dead. But his early experiences and inner drive pushed him in the opposite direction.

Now, armed with a doctorate in education and a deeply personal understanding of students' lives, he pours all his energy into showing kids why school makes sense. As a researcher and motivational expert who chairs the Educational Leadership and Policy Studies department at California State University in Sacramento, Francisco Reveles is quietly revolutionizing how school districts work to engage at-risk students and blunt the impact of gangs. With creative model programs that engage students via the language, values, and role models of their own culture, he's reaching them in ways that a succession of big-ticket government initiatives never have.

Francisco got his start in the gritty barrios of El Paso, Texas, just across the Mexican border from the infamous Ciudad Juarez, "the murder capital of North America." For decades now, the barrio has been a place where the poorest of the poor coexist with drug traffickers and rival gangs.

As a young child, Francisco survived the streets by being affiliated with older gang members and selling newspapers. He witnessed "things children shouldn't see" — acts of violence he still won't talk about. "You had to know the 'code of the streets' if you wanted to stay alive," he says. "You had to have the protection of brothers or cousins; it was survival of the fittest. I was jumped by other kids when I was still in kindergarten, and I'd run the gauntlet to get home every day."

Grinding poverty was the backdrop for everything that went on in the barrios of this border town, like using melon crates for the family dinner table. Or being given a single burrito to eat all day, and then being told to split it three ways with his cousins. Or never being able to afford a doctor. Francisco nearly died once when a badly injured knee became gangrenous.

A turning point came on the day Francisco arrived home to find the family's house being cleaned out by "some nice men wearing ties." They removed his family's few belongings and rolled away his little sister's bicycle while his mother and sisters looked on in stunned helplessness. "I remember the pain in my mom and the anger in my dad," says Francisco. "It was an epiphany. Something changed in me that day. I knew I had to do something to help."

117

He vividly remembers the day he earned a dollar selling newspapers, a good sum for his day's work. "My mother was so happy and proud of me," he says. "I could have used the money to buy food or toys; I bought a new pair of underwear instead. It sounds crazy, but I felt like a million bucks. It was only much later I realized it was my first act of real responsibility and taking care of myself." By the age of nine, Francisco felt like the man of the family, after his father left to find work in California.

But somehow, growing up on the hard-scrabble fringe of America didn't taint his fundamentally positive outlook. "When you live in dire conditions, one of two things happens," Francisco explains. "Either people give up and go under — or they have such a love for life and such intensity that it forges them. They learn to make do with what they have and how to see the good things around them. My parents were like that. As poor as we were, they were resilient. There was the attitude that 'we will get through this.' There was humor and a lot of love."

To Francisco, hard physical labor wasn't a problem. In fact, it was a solution — a way for him to escape the streets and their escalating gang violence. At the age of ten, after his family reunited in a small town in California's agricultural Central Valley, he went from selling papers on the streets to laboring in the fields. One day, his father simply dropped him off at the fields, where he was handed a pair of gloves and a hoe that was too large for his small frame. "I would work all day beside grown men. You drank from the same ladle and you didn't complain; you just kept your mouth shut, even when it was stifling hot in summer," he remembers.

His cheerful, uncomplaining attitude not only kept him going but also attracted unexpected kindness and compassion. He remembers his third-grade teacher, Mrs. Valdez, calling him to her desk to rub lotion on his hands, which were left cracked and bleeding by the hours he spent hawking papers in the chill of winter. He was also helped by some sympathetic Irish nuns, who offered him hot meals and provided a crisp new suit of clothes for his First Communion.

In junior high school, when he lost the family's grocery money on his way to the store, the kindly grocer not only gave him a bag of food but offered him work. The job carried him all through high school, paying his expenses as he blossomed in school. He earned straight As, was quarterback of the football team, competed in track, and became student body president. Encouraged by his teachers, he entered a university-sponsored math contest, winning second prize and a handsome cash award that he gave to his family.

By now Francisco could see the pattern of success in his life. When he did his best, the world opened up to him and good things happened. Upon graduation, he was invited to join not one, but two of the most prestigious military institutions in the United States, the Naval Academy at Annapolis and the Military Academy at West Point. He chose Annapolis, and his town raised the money to get him there. But when a childhood eye injury thwarted his dream of becoming a fighter pilot, he left Annapolis with an honorable discharge.

His appetite for new experiences and challenges next led him to the mountains, where he worked as a wilderness instructor for at-risk Latinos from migrant backgrounds. There he met Reno Taini, founder of the innovative Wilderness School for at-risk teenagers. Something clicked up there in the clear mountain air, as Francisco found the direction for his life's work. "Like Mrs. Valdez back in my childhood, Reno was much more than a teacher," Francisco says. "His intensity was inspiring. He told the kids, 'I didn't bring you up here to the wilderness so you could be second best. Seize the opportunity.' I wanted to share that message with every sad, broken kid I could reach."

Francisco has held onto that passion through his years as a teacher, high-school principal, and university professor. Now he's also highly sought after as an educational consultant working with at-risk teens, parents, and educators. "I want to be that someone who gives kids their hope back," he says. "I want to make sure they understand how wide open their future is, how many good choices they can make, how far they can go. And if they do something good for someone down the road, well, that's the way they can pay me back. All my life I have had great teachers. Now it's my turn."

LESSONS AND INSPIRATION

LIFE IS A FURNACE,
SO KEEP MOVING

Francisco was born into poverty, violence, and discrimination, but his early experiences did not define the trajectory of his life: *"Every experience in life forges you; good or bad, each one legitimizes and validates who you are. How will you respond? Are you resilient, or do you give up? I have always had a great love for life and I know it made a difference. The furnace made me stronger, and there is very little that I fear anymore. I often think, 'Oh, I've been through worse.'"*

YOUR DEMONS CAN BE YOUR MOTIVATORS

"I learned a valuable lesson early on, which is to focus on the positive lessons that were there for me. I did not go with my demons; instead, I used them as my motivators to move ahead. And I think the way I choose to look at my past experiences, as offering something positive and not negative, has helped me all my life."

PAY ATTENTION TO THE BEACONS

"There are people in every life who have an intensity and an interest in who you are. They show up at odd times, and if you're wise, you learn from them. If I've achieved anything, it's because I learned to look for and recognize these people who are like beacons of

light. *And it's true on a larger scale as well. In times of great stress in society, it's the ordinary people who become great teachers. Martin Luther King, Gandhi, Cesar Chavez, and Mother Teresa were all common people who rose up to give great hope to others."*

TO SEE NEW OPPORTUNITIES, CHANGE YOUR VANTAGE POINT

As an avid outdoorsman and wilderness expert, Francisco has taken gang members on mountain trips to teach them about the importance of changing your perspective: *"When you look at the mountain peak, all you can see is a lot of hard work ahead. But once you start climbing, you gain some confidence, and soon the view changes. It's like that in life — in the process of attempting the climb, your horizon changes. If you never attempt it at all, your perspective stays exactly the same, and the options never change. Only by attempting, by pushing beyond what you see right now, will new horizons emerge. You begin to see possibilities — things you want to do, things you can do."*

MAKE YOUR HOPES OPERATIONAL

As a child selling newspapers, Francisco would sometimes look up to see jets from a military base in New Mexico flying high overhead. He wanted to be up there, too, and came close to realizing that dream before it was derailed by an old eye injury.

Even so, says Francisco, *"I learned that you have to back up your dreams with a plan. When I talk to people who are locked up, or in great trouble, they do not want to hear clichés about hope. So I tell them the truth: There is no such thing as a brighter future if you don't have a plan. I call it 'operational hope,' which means hope backed up by a plan to get from point A to point B, and from point B to point C. It's hope laid out in small, achievable steps."*

DON'T TEND TO WOUNDS
YOU DON'T HAVE

"My father taught me a lesson that has saved me a lot of grief in life. He said, 'Even though people may mock you — the way you speak, your hair, your accent, the color of your skin — those are wounds that you don't have to own.' He got me to focus on my own life and not on what others think about me."

IF YOU WANT RESPECT,
START BY RESPECTING YOURSELF

"When I work with groups, I always remind them that if you see yourself as second best, that's how people are going to treat you. And then I ask them, 'If you could be any kind of car, or any kind of animal, what kind would you be?' For cars, they always pick the best. Nobody wants to be a car with four flat tires and busted headlights. When it comes to animals, they want to be a tiger, a cheetah, or a beautiful dove. I tell them, 'You want to be the best, and that's why I'm here.'"

IT'S NOT
JUST ABOUT YOU

"When you focus on something or someone beyond yourself, that's when you can really begin to change," says Francisco. "I started to become a man the day I first contributed financially to the family — to see the happiness in my mom's face is what began to turn me around and pulled me away from the bad elements in my life. When I talk to kids who are locked up, kids who've done some pretty violent things, I don't talk to them through their gang membership. I talk to them through the fact that they are a son, they are a big brother. 'Mijos,' I say, 'which one of you wouldn't lay down his life for his mother or little sister or brother? No matter who you are in life, remember that you don't represent yourself alone. You also represent your familia, your cultura, your nation. You're living for other people, too.'"

SUMMING UP

BY ATTEMPTING THE CLIMB —
WHETHER YOU SUCCEED OR NOT —
YOU CAN CREATE NEW HORIZONS
IN YOUR LIFE.

For more on Francisco Reveles:

Reveles, Francisco. *An Educator's Guide to Latino Gang-Affiliated Youth: Research and Practice*. 2010.

Reveles, Francisco. *Encuentros: Hombre a Hombre (Encounters: Man to Man)*. Sacramento: California Department of Education. 2000.

DVD Latino Youth: From Survival to Success. 2007.

Cada Cabeza Es Un Mundo (Each Mind is a World).
New Mexico: Hispanic Education and Media Group, Inc. 2001.

www.franciscoreveles.com

Author's Note: Francisco Reveles is in the process of acquiring publication and distribution rights to the above-listed materials. Please visit his website for the latest information.

NOW IT'S YOUR TURN TO TRY

Seven Steps to Success

I HOPE the twelve amazing people who've shared their stories in these pages will inspire you. But I'd like to go one important step further: How can *you* apply that inspiration to your own life and what matters most to you?

Working on this book has taught me that there's no single recipe for The Try. But I've also learned that there *is* a practical method you can use to cultivate Try and put it into action, so long as you've got the basic ingredients of discipline and desire. Surveying our Twelve with Try, it's striking to see how many common themes run through their very diverse stories. When you put all the lessons from this book together, they point to seven key steps that can help you realize your goals and ambitions, whatever they may be.

SEVEN STEPS TO SUCCESS:

1 Start with a Dream

2 Turn Your Dream into a Measurable Goal

3 Create a Game Plan and Timetable

4 Make a Commitment

5 Take Full Responsibility

6 Expect Adversity

7 Give It 110%

1 START WITH A DREAM

It's not a matter of what you wish you could achieve. The question to ask is what accomplishment is most important to you — so important that you're willing to put it at the center of your life and make any sacrifice necessary to achieve it. If there's one thing the profiles in this book demonstrate, it's that great accomplishments demand great effort.

Mountain climber Stacy Allison is one person with a lot to say about the power of making a clear choice — *I will do this* — and committing to it totally, once you decide.

Making that kind of commitment is not a casual thing. It's a little like standing at the top of a ski slope that's steeper and bumpier than any run you've ever attempted. So before you take the plunge, get clear right at the start about just what it is you want to accomplish and what tradeoffs and adjustments you're willing to make to get there.

For example, if your goal is a big one, pursuing it will almost certainly leave you with less time for other things, like family and friends, hobbies, music, reading, movies — the list goes on. The Try can lead to a single-mindedness — an almost obsessive sense of purpose — that some people may read as selfishness. It's not for everyone.

But while our Twelve with Try all made sacrifices to do what they did, they also give you the feeling they wouldn't want it any other way. Both Stacy Allison and Jessica Jackley eloquently express how lucky they feel to have found an abiding passion in life.

2 TURN YOUR DREAM INTO A MEASURABLE GOAL

From the early days of his childhood, Ty Murray knew exactly what he was aiming for—to beat the record of his childhood idol, Larry Mahan, by earning seven All-Around World Champion cowboy buckles. Brian Boyle's goal of competing in the Kona Ironman gave him a tangible hurdle, and a way to prove he was "well and whole" after his near-fatal accident. Businessman Jerry Acuff had revenue and profitability targets. Stacy Allison had Everest. Having a tangible, measurable goal not only gave these achievers a clear target to aim for, but also helped them to set up interim goals — in short, a path to their dreams.

It's too easy for ambitions couched in vague, general language like "be a better student" or "start exercising" to dissolve into business as usual. It takes more intention than that to overcome old habits and continual distractions. Instead, resolve to "raise my GPA by a full point" or "finish a half-marathon." Then ask yourself if your goal is realistic, given what it will take and whether you believe you can persevere. In short, have you got the stuff? If a goal seems beyond the realm of possibility, perhaps you can redefine it.

3 CREATE A GAME PLAN AND TIMETABLE

If there's one point on which our Twelve with Try are nearly unanimous, it is the need to break big goals down into smaller steps. Whatever kind of mountain you're trying to climb, it will seem overwhelming if you focus only on the peak. If you break your effort down into steps or interim objectives, you'll be better able to plan how you'll accomplish each one. You'll also set yourself up for a series of small successes to help reinforce your determination.

A critical piece of this is putting your plan into the framework of a timetable. Let others dream of the big things they want to get around to doing "someday." Exactly how are you going to realize your dream, and by when? It may take some research to come up with a viable game plan, and you may need to adjust it based on unforeseen obstacles or events. But you can't have a Plan B if there's no Plan A to start with.

There's a saying that "even the longest journey starts with a single step." In truth, the only way to reach a destination is by putting one foot in front of the other for the entire way. Mapping the journey will help you keep your big goal in sight while staying focused on the next challenge ahead. Hamse Warfa likes to cite one of his favorite quotes: "Those who fail to plan, plan to fail." Operating with that principle helped him go from life as a Somali refugee to testifying before Congress as an expert in conflict resolution.

4 MAKE A COMMITMENT

The Try has power only when you carry it through day by day, moment by moment, so it becomes a driving force behind your thoughts, attitudes, and actions. That's why making and constantly reaffirming a commitment to yourself is key.

Then share your goal with others. That makes you accountable and reinforces your resolve to accomplish what you've announced you will do. Social species that we are, many people are more motivated by the expectations and reactions of others than they are by their own objectives. Declaring your commitment could also bring you support from your family and friends. You may even find surprising offers of help from others you know. Having a cadre of supporters could be just the boost you need.

But don't let it deter you if others don't share your belief in yourself or your enthusiasm for your goal. Many a high achiever has been driven by the desire to prove the skeptics wrong and show the world exactly what he or she can do.

5 TAKE FULL RESPONSIBILITY

It's true that unforeseen events and changing circumstances can affect your game plan and, potentially, the outcome. Elements of luck will certainly play a role. You may find that you have to put your plans on hold temporarily, or regroup and come at your goal a different way. But none of that matters. The success or failure of your effort still rests entirely with you. No excuses! One of Jerry Acuff's favorite mantras echoes what so many other successful people have recognized: "If it's to be, it's up to me."

6 EXPECT ADVERSITY

Carlotta Walls LaNier endured hostility, isolation, and violence as she pursued her goal of graduating from a newly integrated high school. Almost as soon as Jessica Jackley started talking with industry experts about her idea for person-to-person global microlending, they said it would never work. Ann Higdon got a similar reaction to her idea for an electronic smart card replacing food stamps. Jerry Acuff already had a track record as a successful sales executive when he started his own sales consulting firm, only to watch it slide into a sea of red ink. Lexi Alexander saw her first studio film fail miserably at the box office. Stacy Allison was within reach of the summit of K2, the world's second tallest peak, when she gave up the attempt after a team member's fatal accident. Ty Murray's rodeo career was threatened when he sustained one injury after another.

Every single person profiled in this book encountered serious obstacles, setbacks, and failures along the way, and so will you. It's just the nature of things. You're also bound to get negative feedback from people who insist you'll never be able to achieve what you've set out to do. If they have worthwhile points to make, factor them into your planning. Otherwise, ignore the naysayers — or, better yet, channel their negativity to help fuel your determination. Of course, often the biggest challenge is transcending your own doubts about what you can achieve or overcome. Think of it this way: If you don't believe in yourself, why should anyone else?

7 GIVE IT 110%

Say it's the end of the day, you're tired, and you think you've done enough. That's the time to stop, take a deep breath, and ask yourself, "What else can I do today to get one small step closer to my next objective?" That last 10 percent, compounded over time, could mean the difference between success and failure.

If you really want to accomplish something extraordinary, an ordinary effort won't do. You've got to dig deep, give it your all, and then find a way to give a little more.

Does all this sound simple? It's not. If it were easy to become a champion, a successful entrepreneur, or any other kind of role model, everyone would do it. But if you've got the fortitude to keep feeding and growing your own supply of Try, you'll discover that the secret of success is really no secret at all.

For my parting thoughts on this notion of Try, I turn to Dr. E. O. Wilson, the eminent Harvard biologist who is himself an example of Try for his decades-long inquiry into the mysteries of ants and ant behavior. He has also thought and written extensively on sociobiology, biodiversity, conservation, and a host of other topics, twice winning the Pulitzer Prize for nonfiction works. Most recently, he published his first novel, *Anthill*, at the age of eighty! I could not sum up the lessons of *The Try* any more eloquently than he did in these words:

You are capable of more than you know. Choose a goal that seems right for you and strive to be the best, however hard the path. Aim high. Behave honorably. Prepare to be alone at times and to endure failure. Persist! The world needs all you can give.

GUIDE FOR PERSONAL REFLECTION

Your "Seven Steps" Journal

THE TRY is something that comes from within — it's all about your inner drive, focus, and determination. Thinking deeply about these questions may help you take "Seven Steps to Success" in your own life.

1 START WITH A DREAM

Our dreams tell us about who we are at the core — and who we might be if we live up to our potential. They are a way of saying, "Wake up! Live! Make the most of your life!"

1   Do you have a dream — something you could fully commit to doing, becoming, or achieving? If you have several, which one rises to the top?

2   What would you need to give up in order to achieve your dream? How willing are you to make that sacrifice?

3   Write about a time you tried something and failed. What did you learn from that experience?

2 TURN YOUR DREAM INTO A MEASURABLE GOAL

A dream is shadowy and elusive as long as we think of it as "something I wish would happen." It becomes achievable only when we define it clearly as "a goal I will strive for."

4 Why is it important to set goals for yourself?

5 What goal is most important to you at this point in life? Have you defined it in clear, measurable terms?

6 Name a goal you set for yourself in the past. Were you able to achieve it? Why or why not?

7 What are the motivators that will drive you to work toward your goal in the months and years ahead?

3 CREATE A GAME PLAN AND TIMETABLE

Goals can be overwhelming if we focus on the end point. It's easier to make progress if we focus on small steps that move us in the right direction.

8 What is the general timeframe for achieving your goal? Will it take weeks, months, or years?

9 What are the major steps involved? What do you need to do to flesh out your plan?

10 What steps can you take toward your goal right now?

11 Who or what could help you achieve your dream? What knowledge or experience will you need?

4 MAKE A COMMITMENT

It's easy to make commitments inside our heads, where we can let them slide without losing face. It's a lot harder to make a commitment in public, where others may judge us by how well we follow through.

12   Can you think of three or four people with whom you are willing to share your dreams and goals? How supportive or skeptical do you expect them to be?

13   How do you tend to react to people who say you won't be able to accomplish what you've set out to do? Does it undermine or fuel your determination?

14   What could you do to strengthen your resolve in the face of negative reactions from others?

15   What's more important to you: not letting others down, or not letting yourself down?

5 TAKE FULL RESPONSIBILITY

Taking responsibility means looking to yourself for answers when things go wrong and giving yourself credit when things go right.

16   What are some things that could go wrong on your way to accomplishing your goal? Is there something you can do to plan for those obstacles?

17   Think about a time when you faced a difficult problem and tried to solve it on your own. What did you learn?

6 EXPECT ADVERSITY

Almost nothing in life goes exactly the way we want or expect. When things go wrong, some people lose heart while others buckle down and work even harder.

18 What tends to be your first reaction to adversity? What happens after that?

18 What enables someone to make adversity a motivator rather than a stumbling block?

20 Write about a time when you tried hard to accomplish something and were derailed. Thinking back on it, what might you have done differently today?

21 What is it that's really holding you back from achieving what you want in your life?

7 GIVE IT 110%

We all have those times when we can't seem to overcome the obstacles in our way, no matter how hard we work. But the truth is that people often stop short of giving their all, even when pursuing their most cherished dreams.

22   When was the last time you gave something a 110% effort? What were the results, and how did you feel about it?

23   Who are some good role models for giving 110%? What did they accomplish or overcome?

24   What in your life are you willing to give a 110% effort to right now?

GUIDE FOR READING GROUPS

Questions for Discussion

GENERAL DISCUSSION

1   Have there been times in your life when you had The Try? Have there been times when you wished you did?

2   Whom would you point to as an example of The Try in action? (This could be someone you know, or someone you've read or heard about.)

3   What do you think are the most important ingredients of success?

4   Based on your own observations, is it true that "effort often trumps ability"?

5   What do you think is the measure of a successful life? How much does The Try play into it?

6   Is it true that "If you've got The Try, anything is possible"? Why or why not?

7   Are you satisfied with your own supply of Try? Explain.

8   What are some ways that people could increase their supply of Try?

TY MURRAY *page 3*

9   Would Ty's story still be worth telling even if he hadn't met his goal?

10   Do you agree or disagree that "It's the effort, not the outcome, that makes you a winner"? Can you point to an example that reinforces your opinion?

11 Who is another example of someone who models Ty's winning attitude?

LEXI ALEXANDER *page 11*

12 Lexi came to this country with almost no possessions. What assets did she have?

13 Is the power of positive thinking real? If so, where does the power come from?

14 Does everyone have a gift? What are some ways to go about discovering it?

15 What are the best ways to deal with rejection?

STACY ALLISON *page 21*

16 What does Stacy's story tell us about the importance of risk-taking?

17 What techniques can help us to "put fear aside"?

18 What is the upside of failure?

JESSICA JACKLEY *page 31*

19 Why do you think it is that new ideas often run into resistance from the experts?

20 In Jessica's case, was that resistance helpful, or was it just another obstacle to overcome?

21   What are ways to "keep the naysayers in perspective"?

22   What was it that made Jessica unstoppable?

HAMSE WARFA *page 41*

23   How did Hamse's childhood experiences in Somalia shape his progress in the United States?

24   Are leaders born or made? Do you think Hamse would have been a leader had he stayed in Somalia?

25   Hamse talks about how important it was to his family that he succeed in school and contribute financially. How much are you driven by others' expectations versus your own?

ANN HIGDON *page 51*

26   From an early age, Ann refused to see herself as a victim. How do you think that helped her?

27   Do you agree with Ann that "most people only try to be average"? What is the implication for people trying to compete in today's world?

28   Do you think it makes sense to always do your very best at everything you try? Why or why not?

BRIAN BOYLE *page 65*

29   Can you imagine a situation in which you might push yourself like Brian did? What could drive you to do that?

30 Have you ever found good things to come out of something bad that happened to you? What did you learn?

31 What does Brian's story teach us about gratitude?

32 What do you think really drove Brian to enter the Kona Ironman? Could he have accomplished the same thing without taking so much risk?

CARLOTTA WALLS LANIER *page 75*

33 What do you think enabled Carlotta to be one of the few students who stuck it out through graduation?

34 What does it mean to put on "mental armor," as Carlotta did? Have you ever done that? And if so, how?

35 What was Carlotta's sacrifice, and what did she achieve from it? Do you think the results were worth it?

JULIA K. ANDERSON *page 87*

36 What do you think skiing meant to Julia? Was she trying to prove something?

37 Have you ever seen evidence that "the limits you imagine are not real"? Have you ever been surprised at what you (or someone else) were able to do when you really tried?

38 Julia says that, in her experience, the right people tend to show up in her life exactly when she needs them. What do you think about that statement?

39 Julia relies on some practical, day-to-day techniques to counter negative emotions and keep going in spite of her troubles. What techniques like that have you found to be important or helpful in your own life?

SCOTT H. SILVERMAN *page 99*

40 Early in life, Scott was labeled a rebel and a troublemaker. What are some ways his later problems and addictions might have been avoided?

41 Do you agree with Scott's emphasis on service to others? Why do you believe that is, or isn't, important?

42 How can attitude shape a pattern of success?

43 Does Scott's story suggest any ways of improving our public educational and social service systems?

JERRY ACUFF *page 107*

44 What do you think about Jerry's self-education strategy? Why are some people better students in life than in school?

45 Why was Jerry able to keep from labeling himself a failure? Was it a sign of strength, or a symptom of being in denial?

46 What might be the real source of Jerry's charisma?

47 Do you agree with Jerry that "when you give, you get"? How have you seen that operate in your own experiences?

48   On balance, do you see Francisco's barrio origins as being
      more of a disadvantage or more of an advantage for him?

49   What do you think Francisco means when he says, "Life is
      a furnace"?

50   Who are some other people who have turned their demons
      into motivators? What helps make that happen?

51   Do you agree with Francisco that we live not only for
      ourselves, but also for others? How have you seen that
      among your own family and friends?

52   What do you think has enabled Francisco to reach so many
      gang members?

JAMES P. OWEN
A Personal Journey

IT ALL STARTED in 2003, when he saw a movie that changed his life. Troubled by the feeling that something had gone horribly awry in the country he loved, Jim Owen was searching for an answer. A rash of scandals had left corporate America reeling. The spirit of unity that seemed to flower after 9-11 proved chimerical. And the country's culture wars continued unabated.

But one day Jim happened on *Open Range*, the story of cattle-driving cowboys who stand up for what's right against all odds. The film sparked an epiphany: All the laws, all the regulations, and all the corporate ethics manuals in the world don't begin to address the fundamental problem. The missing ingredient, Jim realized, was the clear, unshakable sense of right and wrong that can only come from within.

"I thought back to the cowboy heroes of my child-hood . . . the way they made me want to be better than I was," he recalls, "and suddenly it all clicked for me. The working cowboy, with his code of honor, self-reliance, and courage, was a heroic symbol of everything that had made America great. I wanted to help keep that spirit alive — to do something that, in some small way, would help get our country back on track."

Gripped by a sense of purpose he'd never experienced in his thirty-five-year business career, Jim pondered how to pass on to others the inspiration he now felt. "Coming up with new ways of looking at things, seeing the big picture, commu-nicating that vision — these have always been my best skills," Jim says. "My breakthrough was realizing that integrity and character are things you can't teach, let alone mandate. They can only be inspired."

By the time Jim had framed his ideas under the banner of "Cowboy Ethics," the way forward was clear. He sold his business interest in a successful asset management firm, freeing himself to follow his newfound passion. He began by setting up a new and different kind of venture, reinventing himself as a full-time "entrepreneur of inspiration."

His first step was to assemble a creative team to help him carry out his vision. "There's an old cowboy saying that when you ride alone, you can go fast, but when you ride with others, you can go far. I've taken that to heart," Jim explains. At an age when many of his peers were settling into a genteel retirement, Jim was just getting started. He threw himself into his new career, often waking at 3 or 4 AM to work on new ideas. He also hit the road, engaging audiences all across the country in a dialogue about the values we live by and how they shape the quality of our lives. When businesses, schools, and community groups began talking about ways they might partner with him, Jim knew he had tapped into a deep vein of longing for a more meaningful way of life. Since then, Jim has:

- Authored two books of inspirational photo essays on the Code of the West and its relevance to our lives today. In his best-selling *Cowboy Ethics*, he translated the cowboy code into "Ten Principles to Live By"; well over 125,000 copies have been sold to date. A companion volume, *Cowboy Values*, reflects on the seven core values of the Code of the West and what it means to win at life. It has consistently ranked among Amazon's top-selling books in the motivation category.

- Created a not-for-profit foundation — the Center for Cowboy Ethics and Leadership (www.cowboyethics.org) — to partner with businesses, schools, and organizations in spreading the message that "character counts above all."

- Spoken before more than 200 (and counting) business groups, colleges and universities, school districts, nonprofit organizations, and trade associations all across America.

- Produced a documentary film, *The Code of the West: Alive and Well in Wyoming*. The film spurred the State of Wyoming to adopt legislation making the Code of the West the official State code, an action that garnered coverage in more than 200 media outlets.

- Brought the Code of the West into the classroom, launching a model program for high-school students that was tested for two years in a top Denver public high school and is now being offered to schools across the country.

Now, with publication of *The Try,* Jim is reaching out to an even wider audience with a new theme — one that is cowboy-inspired, but finds heroes in ordinary people operating in widely varied fields of endeavor. "When you think about it, America was built by people who took great pride in their self-reliance, grit, and determination," Jim says. "I hope we haven't lost that can-do spirit. If ever America needed The Try, it's now."

ACKNOWLEDGMENTS

Coming up with great ideas — that's the easy part.
Bringing those great ideas to life isn't so easy.
I'm grateful to all the people who helped make this book a reality.

OUR TWELVE WITH TRY

Ty Murray planted the seed; by sharing your stories of struggle and triumph, all twelve of you helped it blossom and grow. You've given us all a new set of heroes.

THE CORE PROJECT TEAM

BRIGITTE LEBLANC *LeBlanc & Company* — For more than fifteen years, you've been the go-to person for virtually every creative project I've undertaken. I'm proud of what we've accomplished.

MARJI WILKENS *Marji Wilkens Communications* — Your heart and intellect shine through in every story. Welcome to our team!

NITA ALVAREZ *The Alvarez Group, Inc.* — I have never known anyone with deeper awareness or better creative instincts than you. For twenty-five years, you have brought out the best in me.

RANDY GLASS *Randy Glass Studio* — Your skill in rendering a remarkable likeness that also captures someone's spirit is truly amazing.

THE SUPPORTING CAST

KATHRYN MENNONE *Skyhorse Publishing* — You were the true believer — the one who saw the potential in this project and cheered us all on to the finish line.

NICOLE FRAIL *Skyhorse Publishing* — We are grateful for your thoroughness and your delicate touch with the manuscript.

NANCY JAMISON *San Diego Grantmakers* — Thank you so very much for introducing us to some extraordinary people.

ANN MOORE *Cherry Creek High School* — You and your students have taught me that true success is not just what you achieve, but what you overcome.

STANYA OWEN — My partner, my best friend, my sweetheart — after forty-two years together, you continue to amaze me every single day.

J.O.

More Inspiration from Jim Owen

FILMS

THE TRY   If you've enjoyed *The Try* in print, you'll love this 35-minute companion film — great for classroom discussions, assemblies, book groups, or viewing at home. Also available as a specially-priced book and DVD package — perfect for gifting.

CODE OF THE WEST: ALIVE AND WELL IN WYOMING An uplifting celebration of the timeless American spirit and the everyday heroes among us.

BOOKS

COWBOY ETHICS   The book that helped fuel a grassroots movement by translating the unwritten Code of the West into "ten principles to live by."

COWBOY VALUES   Thoughts on our nation's heritage, and why we need it now more than ever. Lushly illustrated with images by some of the American West's foremost photographers.

All book and film profits go to support the work of the nonprofit Center for Cowboy Ethics and Leadership. To order or for more information, visit

WWW.COWBOYETHICS.COM